MW01136420

Praise for Design Profit & Prosper

As someone who has worked with Carina and her designs in the past, she has the wisdom of someone who has studied and worked as a designer. She has wrapped that into this book. It is clear she wants designers everywhere to succeed and it shows through.

-- Sarah Cannon, Marketing
Communications Manager of Sawgrass Ink

Carina is a trailblazer and inspirational leader within the design and business community, and lights the way for any designer wanting to create a successful money-making business from their design work. Her abundance mindset and no holds barred approach to sharing the secrets of her success is a refreshing change to the scarcity mindset and lack of information sharing prevalent within the design industry. Design, Profit and Prosper is gold for any designer wanting to replicate Carina's financial success as a fabric, paper or graphic designer.

-- Simone Bowles, fabric and paper designer

As a successful business owner, I love Carina's down-to-earth approach to helping designers understand both the realistic side and endless possibilities of a design business. Carina's expertise makes her a leader in this space.

-- Kristina Williams, owner Los
Gatos Elite, Los Gatos, Ca

A practical step-by-step guide where Carina gives you the insights, and necessary steps to see real success as a designer. A must have if you're a designer wanting to build a creative business.

-- Diane Rooney, designer

Carina offers a no nonsense approach for designers who want to make money in their business. She is living proof that what she teaches works. This book is a beautiful blend of business "how to" with design expertise. She doesn't hold back and gives new designers the much needed guidance needed to start their business. She sets expectations that every designer needs to hear!

-- Megan Sumrell, Time Management
Expert (and design hobbyist)

It is clear that Carina loves designing and loves her designers. She sets forth clear expectations to help designers everywhere succeed and live their dream careers.

-- Lisa Baldwin, graphic designer

This book is an absolute must-read for designers. I think, unfortunately, that so many creatives think they have to choose between being artists and making money. Carina not only proves that this isn't the case, but she lays out a step-by-step plan for exactly how designers can make their income goals a reality. She has the professional and business-building credits to back up everything she teaches, but her students' track records really cement her expertise. Every designer (and would-be designer) should read this book.

-- Nicki Krawczyk, president of
Nicki K Media, a digital training company, and creator of the
Comprehensive Copywriting Academy

Design, Profit, and Prosper is a gold mine of information that every designer needs to understand how to begin a profitable business.

-- Annette Walter, Founder & Business
Strategist of iEvolve Consulting, CEO of Timber Industries

For the struggling designer, this is a must read! This will help you dig into your own practices to help you achieve the results you need to be a designer who stands out! I have seen Carina work her magic first hand, helping her Design Suite members grow their design talents and make money in their businesses.

-- Abbey Brown, entrepreneur
and owner of the Brownstone and Milestone Market

Carina's expertise makes her a leader in this space and her wisdom is unparalleled. Throughout this book, Carina gives real advice to help designers learn how to make their dreams a possibility.

-- Rachel Perry; business coach,
international speaker, podcast host

This is THE book to make your design dreams a reality and build a profitable and successful business. I love how Carina helps designers think bigger and see possibilities for their business, and then break the path down into clear and actionable advice. It is obvious that Carina is an expert at both design and the business of design.

--Crista Grasso, Lean
Business Scaling Expert, jewelry designer, CEO of Lean Out
Method & Criscara

Giving with her whole heart, Carina provides clear and much needed guidance to make money and be successful in your design business. Her models and advice are invaluable in helping to kickstart and get the most out of your business! I owe so much to her and am grateful for Carina's willingness to share and help others succeed!

-- Julie Thompson, graphic and fabric designer
and owner of Cedar Hill Design Studio

DESIGN PROFIT & PROSPER

A SURFACE PATTERN & CRAFT DESIGNER'S GUIDE TO MAKING MONEY

CARINA GARDNER, PH.D.
FORWARD BY JENNY DOAN

Paperback ISBN: 9798378173259
Hardcover ISBN: 9798378172788

Cover photo by Josh and Carina Gardner

Book and eBook Production by: Ravi Ramgati

For Josh, Siri, Felicity, and Charlie,
the four people I adore and design my life around.

*Carina's 2022 Ciao Bella Collection
for Riley Blake Designs*

Table of Contents

Forward

I am honored to be asked to write the forward for this wonderful book. I started this second career at the age of 50 and while I am not an expert in a lot of things I do know a bit about creating.

Creating is so much more than making things. It is bringing into existence something that did not exist before. It doesn't matter what we create, it matters that we do create. It fills our lives with deep satisfaction and fulfillment.

Creating brings healing and compassion into our life. Creativity grows when your lifestyle supports it and when you can get your hands on the right tools. This book can help steer you in the right direction.

Remember you have to be brave to create, so open your heart, and your mind, set your fears aside. Life is a journey and it is never too late to give it another go. So sit back, relax and let the fun begin!

Jenny Doan
Missouri Star Quilt Company

Carina digitizing a large piece of art

Introduction

Yov have dreamed of using your talents to make beautiful things. You might already know the software or you may just have opened a program for the first time. You may draw, doodle, or lean on the software to help you design. You walk into a store and imagine your products on the shelf. You visualize new product ideas and designs all around you.

But for whatever reason, you have not unlocked how to earn money from your creative work.

Which raises the question:

Is being a profitable designer possible?"

The answer is a resounding "yes."

But the real question you are asking is not if it is possible, but rather "Is it possible *for me?*"

If you will make some changes in the way you think about design and the design industry, the answer is still a resounding "yes."

Your unique perspective and creativity are the cornerstone to your aspiring career as a designer. However, most aspiring designers do not understand many of the foundational steps needed to become profitable. This book gives you all of the strategies you need so *you* can prosper.

I believe anyone can break through as a designer because of my own winding journey. I was never the top artist at school. Innate talent seemed to elude me as a teenager. However, I *was* creative. I knew I was good at generating solutions. Like many of you, I also had that certain spark of ingenuity important to being a designer.

If this sounds like you, you will love this book. Whether you call yourself an artist, creative, crafter, quilter, or designer, my goal is to help you understand how to propel yourself into the world of design.

As you are reading this book, you will see that I draw from my own experiences to help you create a design life that makes sense for you. Because of that, I need to clarify that I am a fabric, paper, and craft designer. This is also sometimes called surface pattern design.

While many principles I am writing about apply to other industries and design niches, this book helps those interested in the areas of design I have been successful in.

One of my personal missions is teaching technical and strategic skills that will make women financially free. I was able to teach design skills at a university. I was able to teach strategic and marketing skills as a creative director at a major company. My goal is to meld the two to help women live their creative dreams *and* be profitable.

I hope you enjoy this book. But I hope more that you will *do* the things I teach you in this book. I try to lead by example, and if you were one of my designers, these are some things I would advise you to do to create the business of your dreams.

Finally, because this book helps you discover your design journey, I made you a corresponding workbook you can download for free. I would love for you to have your own moments of clarity as you explore how to make money as a designer as you read this book. Download the workbook at www.designprofitprosperbook.com as my gift to you.

Enjoy!

CHAPTER 1

IT'S NOT THAT KIND OF DESIGN BOOK

I did not grow up with a lot of money. My dad was raised in a tiny town in Idaho where the most famous thing to ever happen was the filming of the Napoleon Dynamite movie. He was the second youngest of nine children and the first to get a college degree. My Chinese mom was an immigrant from Malaysia. She came from a different culture and from poverty I still do not quite understand.

When I was five, our family moved to a town in Tennessee. My mom made homemade bread—which I now miss terribly—because we didn't have enough money for store-bought bread. I also only wore second-hand clothing despite being the oldest child. I did not know we had very little money until the seventh grade. That's because in seventh grade, our family moved, and I began attending a new school. It was there I learned my clothing wasn't like the other kids'.

That same year, I asked my mom for something new, like *from-the-store* new. She bought me a $12 shirt from Walmart, which I bought two sizes too big so it would last me a long time. For a kid who had nothing new, I was incredibly proud of my new shirt.

Of course, one new shirt just showed me how old all the other things I owned were. So all this purchase did was make me *more* aware of what I did not have.

As middle school became high school, I became more and more aware of how little money our family had. I hated to ask for any money for school fees for clubs or activities. I did not go to my cross country awards banquet because I did not know and did not want to ask if we had the money to pay for a dinner out for the ceremony. Eating out was just something we did not do.

Our family did have enough to clothe, shelter, and feed us. While it felt tight and I could feel the strain of limited resources, I always had enough food and clothing to make it through.

I only tell you a little bit about this background because I know many design books out there will tell you how to design well. These books help you become a skilled designer by teaching you typography, history, and design elements.

This is not that kind of design book.

I have taught designers as a professor while working on my Ph.D., as a creative director of a large scrapbooking company, as the president of a kids company, and now in my design program, Design Suite.

The piece of advice designers ask me repeatedly is, "How do I make money?"

They do not ask how to become the best designer in the world. They do not ask how to level up their Illustrator knowledge. They want to understand *how to make money.*

I am sensitive to this desire because of my background, which is why I shared it with you. It's not for you to feel sorry for me. In fact, it is to help you understand that *I understand where you are coming from.*

I started my design business to provide income for my family. As a professor or creative director, I was limited by a salary. As a design business owner, the sky was *and is* the limit. I found out quickly that money was a vehicle for making life a little bit easier.

I feel strongly that by teaching you the basics of making money as a designer, life will get a little easier for you too.

In Jenny Doan's book "How to Stitch An American Dream" I love that she calls herself a "utilitarian quilter." If I had to give myself an adjective, it would be "practical designer."

Here's why.

As a practical designer, instead of focusing on what *I* think would be fun to make, I focus on what *my customers want me to make them.* Most aspiring designers come from the opposite viewpoint. These designers have a dream of creating fabric collections, scrapbooking lines, and art in their own unique style. That viewpoint focuses on the *designer's wishes*, not the customers'.

Practicality is how I have built a design business that continues to be profitable. If you choose to be practical, not only will you be able to be creative, but you will be able to support yourself financially.

A Designer Who Cares About Customers

If you are a designer who wants the big dream and lifestyle of a designer, it is absolutely within your grasp. You must make shifts in the way you design and why you design. I will give you three models to work from so you can achieve those dreams. These models are called "Good Better Best," "The Design Process," and "The Three Hurdles."

But before we get to that, you need to make a major shift in your design business thinking. This shift needs to be about becoming a designer who cares about your customers.

So while I have talked quite a bit about being profitable, the real focus for a money-making designer isn't necessarily profitability. It is actually creating recurring value for your customers.

The irony is that many of you *are* your own customer! You *are* the fabric buyer, die-cut file buyer, and font buyer. Because of this, you already have many of the tools and insights about how you would like to purchase designs and use designs.

Think logically about what products you enjoy purchasing, why you purchased them, and how you used them. What made those products different? Why did you buy them? Once you know that, you can think about bringing great products to your customers.

I have made and cut thousands of craft projects as a die-cut designer. One year, we had so many 3D projects that my team created the "graveyard." The graveyard was a corner of our office that consisted of boxes of finished 3D projects, printouts, scrapbooking albums, and samples from new products.

We tested our products because we wanted to make sure that they worked. I did not want a customer to be unhappy with one of those products. I also created instructional posts for many projects or videos on my YouTube channel. They weren't created because I thought they would be fun. They were created because I hoped a crafter would find them useful for their creative process.

I have built a very functional design business, which is why I am a practical designer. Practical designers make designs that matter to customers and can be used. They design products with the end user in mind. These designers test their products until they know they work. They aren't afraid to try new products to see if customers like them. They are always seeking new strategies and ways to make revenue.

I should be clear that in the past I have not always been a practical designer. I started a kids company where my focus was on the product, not necessarily on finding a real opportunity in the marketplace. That company would have been far more successful had I followed my own advice in this book. I did not spend enough time on differentiation and how the product would be more useful to the customer.

If you have struggled to make money as a designer, it is not because you are not a good designer. I suspect your artwork is wonderful. If you are an aspiring designer and getting started, your artwork will grow with time and experience. The number one design business problem that each designer faces is making money, and it all starts with thinking about your customer.

If we can change how we think about creating products, we will also solve the profitability problem. To state it simply:

*New designers think they should develop products for the sake of creation and beauty. The artwork is **self-serving**. Practical designers develop products to help customers solve problems and strive to create differently so they stand out. The artwork is insightful and **selfless**.*

The difference between these types of designers is more clearly understood from the words and phrases they use. The self-serving and often unprofitable designer will say something like, "I could make something that good!" Whereas the customer-focused designer says, "I could make something different and unique that stands out."

What would the world look like if every designer strived to make something "just as good as" what was already out there? I can tell you it would be more bland, more predictable, and even a little heartless. However, the designer who finds the intersection where their unique style and the customers' value of their artwork meet will find fulfillment in this career.

If you are an aspiring designer trying to figure out how to start a design business, this creative career often seems like a fun adventure in creativity, drawing, and color manipulation. While design is all of those things, a profitable design career also requires key ingredients I never taught as a professor. And here's the thing, I didn't learn these key ingredients from learning or teaching at a university; I learned them from running a design business. My experience as a freelancer, digital product designer, creative director, as the owner of my own physical product company, and designing for manufacturers has changed my view over time about what it means to be a designer.

That's why I am now a practical designer, and you should be too.

When I taught college, design was about creating beautiful and functional solutions. It was about teaching students how to create a focal point and matching the right fonts together. This fits the "Designer's Style" needed to find the sweet spot.

When I was a creative director, it was about creating what sold, what customers wanted, how the product was used, and how it was showcased. This is an example of finding 'Customer Value" needed to find the sweet spot.

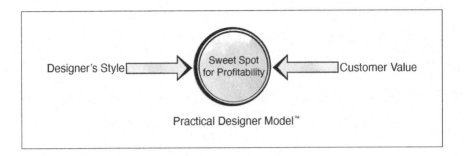

Practical Designer Model™

When I was a president of a kids company, it was about understanding the marketing of a product, knowing the key markets to place the product, knowing when to quit trying to make a product work, and when to print more of another. I tried to use both "Designer Style" and "Customer Value" to find that sweet spot.

Now that I teach design again, these different experiences have shown me the easiest and hardest paths to making money as a designer. It also taught me that design is much more than the colors and fonts you choose for a project. It is about whether your work will *sell* and provide a solution for a customer.

These experiences helped me build the models and advice in this book, which I tried to keep short and concise. I draw from my personal experiences so you can see that it is possible to be profitable. As a designer, I like getting information efficiently and effectively to implement. I hope you do too.

You can create a design business a million ways. What I focus on are the tactics I find the best for creating a long-term, profitable business. Take the three models in this book and apply them to your current or new business so that you can prosper.

One last thing: I am not only a practical designer but a realist. I wish I could tell you that designing was going to be all lollipops and rainbows. Unfortunately, it will not be.

You WILL have lots of amazing magical moments of creation, so be excited about that. But also be excited for the hard work and growth you will experience as a design business owner. Both make this endeavor an exciting and fun one!

Ask my design students about my obsession with giving them a reality check about owning a design business and they will tell you I will happily give the tough love. Knowing the hardships and realities will make you the profitable designer you truly desire to be. Doing the hard work and making mistakes are part of the process.

Closely assess the models in this book and analyze where you fall short. By doing so, you will see the holes in your own business. This process will help you think of ways to fill those holes.

After spending so much time helping new designers become profitable and build income-generating design businesses, I know anyone can become a successful designer. It requires more grit, determination, self-awareness, and creativity than most people think but *you* can be one of those people. So let's begin.

Note: As a reminder, go to www.designprofitprosperbook.com for a free coordinating, downloadable workbook. Take your own design business through the models by using this book with the workbook.

CHAPTER 2
I HAD TO MAKE MONEY

Designing was never in my early career plans. It was something that, thankfully, happened to me.

While in college, I had every intention of going into advertising. I had studied Ogilvy, McCann, and other advertisers while working on my Communications degree. The advertising world appeared creative, sexy, and so cool to this small-town Tennessee girl.

Then everything changed.

During my final year in my Communications program, I was introduced to a software called Photoshop. I had an advertising project to make swimming pools seem awesome in Utah, even though they could not be used year-round.

I envisioned an advertisement of a woman lounging in a hot tub or heated pool with a range of mountains behind her. When I talked to my advertising professor about this, he suggested I go to the design college computer lab to create this imagined image in Photoshop.

Now, during almost everyone's design journey, they have their first meeting with the softwares that we use in the industry. Those first rendezvouses are often full of tears, frustration, and sometimes even joy. I had that first experience walking into that college computer lab all those years ago. Wrestling with Photoshop and bending it to my will during that project made my teeth grind in vexation. I had to repeatedly sign up for one-hour time slots in the college computer lab. Because I was facing a deadline in my advertising class, it was a short time frame for learning this new software.

Through the tears, one thing became very clear. I realized that the person who controlled the images also controlled the real message of an advertisement. The colors, placement of the type, photo, and headline font were important. Since the designer created these elements and the *placement* of these elements, the designer had ultimate control of the final message.

I decided I needed more education around design to become a better advertiser. So as soon as I finished my Bachelor's degree, I moved with my husband to Minnesota to begin a Master's program in design.

A few months into my Master's degree, it became clear that design was so much bigger and, dare I say, so much more *fun* than advertising alone. My focus moved completely to design.

While in school, I audited core courses I had missed as an undergraduate, like graphic design foundations, graphic design history, and typography. I eventually went on to teach or TA these courses when I started my doctorate.

The time spent as a graduate student in design opened my eyes to an important principle I had not been exposed to before. This principle was that *design could be learned*.

This was a shift from what I assumed about artists and designers growing up. I thought that these were innately gifted people. That they were the select talented chosen ones. However, as I delved into the world of design, I saw that a student could be taught the core principles. Through discipline and practice, design could be cultivated into a talent.

This life-changing concept pushed me further as a designer, especially as I saw technology blossom for those who felt like mediocre drawers. I watched my freshman designers grow into capable, skilled designers in their junior and senior years. This pattern showed me that learning design was a *repeatable* process. I knew I was not the only one able to learn this creative skill.

The Pursuit of Business

It is one thing to become a designer in order to start a career at a company or corporation. It is quite another to build a design business. At the university, coursework was built to teach students to become good designers that would go on to design for *companies*. Even though some would build freelance businesses, teaching marketing and sales was not a part of the university curriculum. Instead it focused on creating outstanding designers.

So when I finished my doctorate and built my own design business, I ran into some massive problems. The first was that just because I was a good designer didn't mean I understood

1. How to sell my designs or

2. How to make stuff customers wanted.

Understanding these two concepts became fundamental to building a successful design business.

Looking back, ignorance was bliss. My first year as a design business owner was fraught with mistakes. I had decided to start my business by designing and selling digital scrapbooking designs.

I juggled my young family, website design, customer acquisition, and product development. To be clear, this was back when website design included writing HTML code from a Dreamweaver book. Customer acquisition included chatting in forums since many of the advertising avenues we use today did not exist. Everything felt hard because it *was* hard.

After nearly 11 months, I had made very little money. The 200-plus products I had designed went unpurchased. The painful, money-less months gave me several "aha" moments. Here are a few those ahas:

Hint, if you are currently selling products and are struggling, I highly recommend you take this list and see if it applies to your current circumstances.

1. I was trying to build an audience while spending most of my time designing. It was not working.

2. Much of what I was designing wasn't appealing to customers. Why? Because I wasn't a digital scrapbooker to begin with. More on this in Chapter 2.

3. Being a good designer and building a good product was not enough.

After struggling for eleven months, someone told me about a well-known scrapbooking website that was starting a digital scrapbooking shop. I applied to that shop, hoping and praying I would somehow make sales.

Guess what? During my first month in that digital scrapbooking shop, I made the same amount of money I had made during the eleven months in my own shop. Wow!

As the months went on, I made more money each month in that digital shop and landed several contracts.

What were my takeaways from that?

1. That audience building at the same time as starting a design business was a waste of time. This is because audience build requires time and expertise similar to being a designer. I did not have time to be both the product builder *and* the marketing expert.

2. That there were certain designs customers liked better than others and that I should learn from to the winning designs.

3. Being a good designer on your own little design island is a major disadvantage. I needed a bigger network to get key information.

Why You Should Be Excited

I have talked to hundreds, if not thousands, of designers. Some I taught while others were under my creative direction. There is a similar underlying story that comes up again and again.

This story has all the elements of a tragic plot line. The aspiring designer creates something. It doesn't sell. They try something else. It is more interesting or more intricate. It also doesn't sell; worse, it sells just enough to make you continue half-heartedly. Finally, the designer gives up because they are stuck and unsure how to move forward.

This is because they are living their dream of designing, but without *sales,* they feel like a failure.

If this sounds vaguely familiar, fortunately, you are not alone. Most aspiring designers have gone through this journey. What I do not want is for you to get stuck in this sad plot line. We know of artists who have stayed in this story, and it did not end so well for them. And yes, I am referring to examples like Van Gogh.

When I advise designers in this scenario, I ask them if they learned anything from the failed attempts. Most say they questioned their abilities as an artist or a designer. Others say they didn't know what to do, so they stopped taking action. Most felt like failures. Many felt that the path ahead was foggy and confusing.

To those designers, I would implore you to look carefully at all of your actions thus far. Only after this self-reflection is it time to assess what is next.

For example, when I had made very few sales in my first month as a digital scrapbooking designer, I determined I needed more products to sell to test colors, themes, and patterns. So my *action* was to make more products.

When some of those products sold, I could identify my best sellers. My next action was to make more products like the ones already selling. I was my own marketing research firm trying to understand what customers' liked.

When I found it was the same five people buying my designs, my next action was to spend more time audience building to find more people to come to my website.

Notice how every time I ran into a problem, I looked for a solution and took action?

Sometimes these solutions worked. Other times I was back to the drawing board. Either way, I always created new actions.

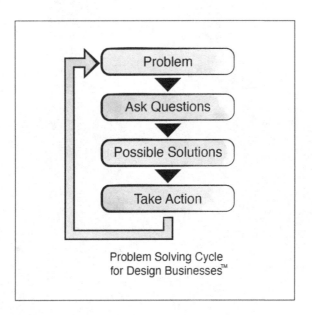

Problem Solving Cycle
for Design Businesses™

The problem solving cycle above is a sequence of events that occur on a daily basis in my business. Some might even think it is basic. However, after teaching thousands of designers over the years, it is clear that most designers just need to do the simple steps outlines in the cycle to get their businesses to work. While most can identify the problem, few will bother to come up with solutions and take action.

Building a design business involves getting into the details of the *struggles* of your design business. Identifying multiple solutions and taking action is the only way to know whether the design business you are building will be profitable. If you can get good at that, your business will take a turn for the better.

*Problem solving includes learning
how to use your own products.*

This should be an exciting revelation for those who do not mind doing the work. You are less stuck than you realize. It's time to get real about what you are doing right and what you could do better.

A great example is the early years of my own design business. I realized over the eleven months that audience building was not my strength. So instead, I dug into the thing I was good at—designing. The solution to my audience building problem was to find a shop that already had an audience. Whoa! Sales started pouring in.

Sales of your design work is the *number one objective* of your design business. For me, finding sales was not an option. It was necessary for me to make money. I had a mountain of student loan debt, two small children, and a husband also in school.

Because I had to make money, it drove me to pivot quickly and effectively in my business.

Some artists or designers out there will tell you, you should learn design or art for the fun of it. If that is your intent, then it is a hobby, which by the way is one-hundred percent fine. My mom is a phenomenal watercolorist and has no intention of selling her work. It's just her passion.

However, if you want to turn your passion into a business, it turns out that *sales* is the missing element. Sales are about as unsexy and scary to a designer as it gets. However, it also differentiates your business from a hobby.

So What's Next?

As designers, we aim to make the world a more visually stimulating place *while* generating income. This can only happen if customers *want* what you make.

As I guide you through becoming a better designer and a solution builder, question what you are doing or what you want to accomplish along the way. It will open your eyes to how to build an amazing design business.

I cannot emphasize enough that design is a journey of self-discovery and implementation. With this in mind, remember to download your free workbook at www.designprofitprosperbook.com.

This workbook will ask you more questions about your current or future design business to help you determine your next action steps. By writing down what you are doing, as the workbook asks you to do, you can also take action on what you are not yet doing.

 # CHAPTER 3

YOUR PAST

I shared some of my past with you because I wanted you to understand why I felt that money is an important piece of the design business puzzle. For some creatives, making art or feeling fulfillment may be the most important. For me, all the things—money, art, and fulfillment—play key roles in creating a successful design business.

When I was in graduate school, I took a screen printing class. Screen printing is pushing ink through a fine screen to create an image. For every color, you need a separate screen, so the more complex the image, the more screens you have to create.

I was excited about this class. I did not need it for graduation so I audited it so I could work on my own projects.

I started with a particular image that required about five screens. Based on watching the professor during the process, it looked easy.

I passed the color through a single screen to start the image. This was a thick black stroke line of the main image. When I passed the second color through the screen, I was dismayed because it was not within the stroke lines! It was off by about a quarter of an inch and looked terrible. Worse, I had three more screens to go and the mistake required me to start over again.

The cool thing about screen printing is that it is easy to create several prints at once. So I cleaned my screens and started a fresh print.

Once again, I was slightly off during the inking process. It wasn't quite as bad as the first print, so I decided to go ahead and put on the third, fourth, and fifth screens. The more colors I added, the more out of alignment things became, and the more off the entire print looked. I know some screen printers like this look, but this was not the look I was going for.

I practiced about twenty prints, and towards the end, I got better at lining up the screens.

It's easy to look back at the process and recognize that executing a new art technique was going to require practice. The hands-on experience would help me understand how to make the *next* print correctly.

For the next screen printing project, not only did I do tremendously better, but I had more screens and was much more precise. My execution was better because I had more experience.

Just like the screen printing process, our past experiences help us know how to navigate our future. My understanding of the screen printing process helped me identify my strengths in the process as well as my weaknesses. Experiencing the process made it easy for me to know how to move forward to excel.

The next section is broken down into possible "past experiences" that you have had. Your past experience brings the skills, beliefs, and attitudes that help and hinder the process of creating a profitable design business.

Identify if these backgrounds relate to your current state. Determine what strengths and weaknesses you bring to your design business.

Graphic Designers

I started my design business as a graphic designer, so I understand the good, bad, and ugly from this experience. I leaped into creating my own business because I knew I had the skills to create amazing products. But as you read in the last chapter, I didn't understand how sales worked.

I have a program called Design Suite, where I attract many people with graphic design degrees. These designers have been classically trained, which means they understand design vocabulary, how to create beautiful work, and are proficient in the software.

Just like when I started a design business, they do not understand sales. Some do not understand design production. Most do not understand the field they are making products in. Few have the industry contacts they need to find success.

My husband always jokes that the first few digital scrapbooking products I made were horrendous. I take no offense because he is right. How could I make good products even if I had great design skills when I didn't understand the digital scrapbooker and what she liked?

The main strength of my graphic designers who are trying to move into the surface pattern or craft industries is their abundance of skills. Their biggest weakness is not understanding the customer.

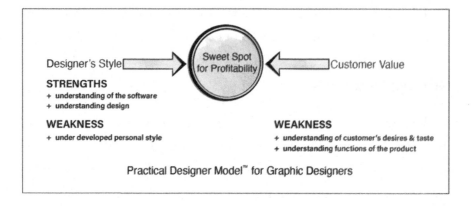

Practical Designer Model™ for Graphic Designers

If graphic designers can go into this niche field of design (or any niche within the field of design) with an open mind, they will find that their training will serve them well. My recommendations for graphic designers are the following.

Graphic Designers -
Do your research and become the customer.

When I got started, I did not understand which papers were popular with customers because I was not behaving like the customer. Once I realized this, I started creating digital scrapbooking layouts for an album I made for my family.

Only when I did that did I realize what digital scrapbookers liked and didn't like using. If I could not use a paper in my own digital scrapbooking album, I threw it out. How would any of my customers use it if I would not use it?

Graphic Designers - There is more to learn.

I run into many graphic designers with university degrees who believe they know everything about design. It's another sign of their inexperience. As a previous professor of design, a creative director, and business owner, I know I do NOT know it all. Things I thought I would never do, for example like using a drop shadow, become necessary in certain design situations. While you might not catch me using Comic Sans any time soon, experience after college is the best teacher for graphic designers.

I recently talked to a designer interested in my program who said they did not need the coursework because they had a graphic design degree. I asked if they understood how to build a fabric collection for a quilting company correctly. They answered they thought they could figure it out. I asked if they understood the die-cutting software's production layout. They did not but hoped that the Internet would provide an answer. I inquired deeper still and realized this designer relied on their degree and *not* their experience to get them the best result.

As someone who has multiple degrees, I know that what taught me the most to be a great designer is my business experience and not my degrees.

With niche design industries, graphic designers must start much of their education over again. They will have a jump start on the software and great design principles. However, understanding the customer, printing methods, sales strategies, and new production techniques are what turns a graphic design degree graduate into an exceptional design business owner. These things happen *after* graduation and come only with experience.

Crafters, Quilters, Sewers, and Creatives

Creatives like crafters, quilters, and sewers have the opposite problem of graphic designers. They understand the customer well because they *are* the customer. In boot camps and workshops I teach, I often tell people to build their customer avatar around them self. Why? Because experience as a crafter or quilter is a powerful asset when it comes to understanding the customer.

Crafters and sewers have been immersed in their hobby for years if not decades. A quilter collecting and sewing fabrics for years will know what fabric sizes are best, what colors work together, or what is trending. A crafter who builds houses and flowers with their die-cutting machine will have created using hundreds of purchased files. Crafters understand what cuts well, how to incorporate ribbon, or how to best use a stamp. They also know when a file does not *cut* well and how frustrating that can be.

When I was a new die-cut designer, I cut out everything. I was also the Creative Director of a large scrapbooking company, so I liked to cut everything in paper. I once sent a design through my machine over ten times in total frustration on a specific project I was working on. I finally decided that if I was frustrated cutting this, my customers would be as frustrated. I returned to the design process and reworked the file so that it would cut well on the first pass.

I love working with crafters and sewers because they understand things about the market that a classically trained designer does not. A creative comes with a unique perspective that can often be directed into a profitable niche.

The weakness of the crafter or sewer is that they do not have design skills, vocabulary, or knowledge of the software. Getting those skills are a necessary part of a crafter/sewer's evolution into a full-fledged designer.

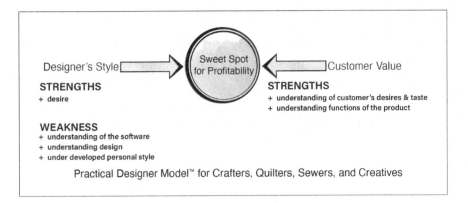

Practical Designer Model™ for Crafters, Quilters, Sewers, and Creatives

Here are recommendations I have for those starting here.

Crafters, Quilters, Sewers, and Creatives - You are not behind.

Because crafters, quilters, and creatives come from a hobby, they immediately feel they are behind in the design process. I always ask, "How are you behind, and who are you comparing yourself to?"

There is no such thing as being *behind*.

You are starting a new journey and are exactly where you are supposed to be. Those with a graphic design degree spent four years learning software and design principles. Creatives may have to spend the same amount of time and effort learning the software and principles. This does not leave you behind. Your journey has begun.

Learn to manage your expectations around this and you will be much happier as you build your amazing design business.

Crafters, Quilters, Sewers, and Creatives -
Be open to technology.

Being open to learning lots of new software and giving yourself the time to play is essential to living your dream career. I have several creatives in my Design Suite program and love working with them because of their enthusiasm for becoming a designer. Use that excitement to learn the technology. Don't be afraid to make mistakes or make imperfect designs.

I also want to normalize the frustration you might have with the software. As I stated before, I cried plenty when I got started with learning Photoshop for the first time. This is a normal part of learning a new technology. By simply designing every day, you will become better and better. You will also be a lot less frustrated. Use experience and time to make technology your friend.

Illustrators and Artists

I love illustrators and artists because they have a keen sense of their own art and style. This is a major strength because they usually have confidence that can lead them on the path towards generating sales. They are also practicing their illustration and artistic skills daily, which helps them become strong action-takers.

The main weakness of the artists is learning to digitize those designs so the art is commercialized. There is also often a struggle to understand sales outside of a traditional art gallery setting.

For the artists I work with, learning the software and understanding how to make the product palatable for the customer is one of their main learning curves. There is sometimes resistance to doing what a customer likes versus what the artist desires to create.

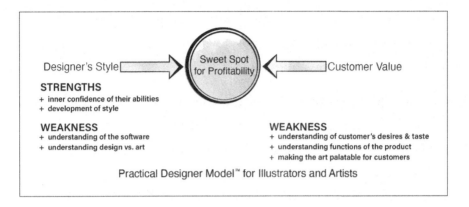

Practical Designer Model™ for Illustrators and Artists

Here are some of my suggestions for illustrators and artists.

Illustrators and Artists -
Be open to changing your art to meet market demands.

One of the coolest things about artists is that they have a confidence about their art that I admire. That confidence actually helps with the sales process. What it does not help with is the adaptability process. (And by the way, if you don't feel like a confident artist, keep reading! There's info for you below.)

I always suggest that as a designer uploads products into the marketplace, that a good business owner will analyze what is selling and make *more* of that item. However, if an artist gives in to their natural inclination to "make art" they sometimes ignore the practicality of giving customers *more* of what they want.

Learn to make your art adaptable to market demands. That is how you will get more sales and build a profitable business.

Illustrators and Artists - When you aren't confident

I sometimes meet illustrators and artists who are not confident in their art. This lack of confidence may reach deep into their childhood when their art wasn't accepted by a teacher, parent, family member, or friend. Debunking beliefs around what is "good" art is difficult but necessary for running a business.

How do I know this? Because the sales process requires *vulnerability*. That means putting a price on our art and allowing customers to see it. I have seen several designers and artists put their work up and, within an hour, pull it back down again. Some of you are nodding your head as you read this because this is you.

You will need to work on confidence so you can get better at being vulnerable and allowing others to buy from you.

Other Creatives

I work with women who used to be landscape architects, fashion designers, and interior designers. If this sounds like you, you bring an immeasurable knowledge to the surface pattern design industry. Many come with a little software knowledge but need to brush up or go deeper. Many come with a strong eye for design and detail.

Whatever your journey or where you come from, consider your strengths and weaknesses. Don't discount what you can accomplish because the experience you bring to the table gives you a unique perspective that can add a lot to the industry.

Beliefs

I mentioned before that my Bachelor's degree is in Communications. So why wasn't it in design or art if I felt so creative? It is because I never felt I was a good enough *artist*, so I never applied to an art program.

I used to believe in the starving artist myth. I thought that by becoming an artist I was doomed to make no money—cue that Van

Gogh reference again. Seeing as he has come up twice in the first three chapters, I think I might have a complex.

Our beliefs about ourselves and the world can propel or freeze our actions. Just as I did not bother applying to the art program in college, I bet many of you have avoided some much-needed actions. Some of these might be learning the software or paying for a more in-depth design education.

Here are a few beliefs I hear from aspiring designers. They do not even realize these beliefs are controlling their actions.

- There is not a way to make money as a designer.

- The software is too hard to learn.

- The market is over saturated with too many designers already.

- I'm not a good enough artist.

- No one will like my designs.

- I'm not interesting or different enough for anyone to buy my designs.

There are numerous beliefs that hold people back from living their best creative life, but these are among the most damaging. Determine why you hold the beliefs you have and question them all.

Here are beliefs that I have seen propel designers forward:

- I am a solution builder.

- I can figure out ways to get more information and education.

- I know that I am unique.

- The right people will like my designs.

- I can learn the software if I just practice every day.

- I know my designs will rise above in this market

- I will invest time and money in my design business.

Find out what beliefs are controlling your actions. If you have not learned the software, is it because you are worried about not creating perfect designs or failing to recreate what is in your mind? If you are not looking for avenues to sell your designs, is it because you are attached to the art-making or design process and unwilling to get vulnerable enough to allow others to see your work?

Find out what is holding you back. That is the only way to change your actions.

Confidence

Put me in a room with two equally talented designers and I can tell you exactly which one will build a competent design business.

Which will build that profitable design business? It is always the one with confidence that they can do it, but the humility to ask for help.

And if that is true, then design isn't just about being the "best designer" in the room. That is because I know that the "best designer" in the room is not always the one that is the most successful.

Why is the confident designer more likely to create a money-making business?

It is because confidence produces action and humility inspires curiosity and learning.

Some people come with confidence while others need to develop it. Here's a great example. As a two-year-old, one of my daughters would climb the kitchen counter behind my back to get herself a cup of water. This always threw me for a loop because her older sister would never climb the counter but instead ask politely for a drink. This toddler was confident that she could get what she wanted when she needed it and created the action. She did not wait to ask.

Are you waiting for someone to tell you that you are good enough? Maybe that you are creative enough? Or maybe you are waiting to be discovered? Perhaps that is why you are not creating the action necessary to become a profitable designer.

Here is the cool thing. If you lack confidence, do not despair. Confidence can be built with skill and community, *just like design.*

Do you see a theme here? Design is learned. Confidence is learned.

So are you ready to learn a little more so we can build up your understanding of design and confidence?

Carina's 2013 Homemade with Love Collection for Cartabella

CHAPTER 4
GOOD BETTER BEST

One of the first classes I took as a budding designer was Graphic Design History. My eyes hurt that entire semester. It was because I saw art in an entirely new way. Some of the art movements I liked. Others I detested. All were interesting and changed the way I saw art.

One of my favorite movements was the Arts and Crafts Movement headed by William Morris. Morris said, "Have nothing in your house that you do not know to be useful or believe to be beautiful."

I love that sentiment because it applies well to any design business. Customers will happily buy the value you have created in creating beautiful and functional pieces.

A design business should be centered on creating *valuable* products. The more beautiful and unique they are, the better these products will differentiate you.

In this chapter, I want to concentrate on creating great designs. This is the core of becoming a designer because sales will not happen if you do not have great designs. Notice I did not say "perfect" designs. That's because, as you will see with this model, we are always striving towards "better' not perfect.

Good Better Best

I used to teach a lesson called "Good Better Best." I would show a scrapbooking paper that was pretty "good". There was nothing wrong or blatantly bad about the design.

Then I would show a "better" paper design. It was clearly more designerly with clean lines, coherent negative space, and maybe some better design elements.

The final scrapbooking paper I showed was always the best. The "best" paper went beyond the "better" paper because it considered function and market. Sometimes it was because the design was unique or more intricate. Sometimes it was because the *purpose* was clearer to the customer. The best designs always have more meaning and reasoning behind them.

Here's a fabric example. A "good" textile design will be laid out nicely with a pretty element or two. The colors are pleasing, and there is nothing wrong with the design. A "better" textile design will incorporate more elements or make the overall shape more pleasing. The "best" design further pushes the shape, adds more details, and changes the scale. The scale change accommodates quilters who want to cut this textile into smaller pieces.

Good   Better   Best

Damask from Ciao Bella Fabric Collection
by Carina Gardner for Riley Blake Designs

The example above is a damask from my Ciao Bella collection that I created for Riley Blake Designs. The progression above shows all the stages I went through to create the best version of the damask.

The Model

In a world where anyone can become a designer, professional designers differentiate from amateurs by way of design knowledge, mentorship, thoughtfulness, and experience.

The Good Better Best Model shows the stages for creating your best design. What makes something better or best is how a designer pushes a design. They ask questions about functionality and intricacy. My Good Better Best Model will help you think about your designs in a new light.

Good Better Best Model™

Good

"Good" is what it sounds like. The design rarely has anything inherently wrong with it. It is fine. As designers, having a bunch of *fine* designs is not what we are going for.

Good designs are often characterized by understanding the software and its capabilities. Good designs are typically produced by designers who have created something with their newfound design software skills. Good designs may or may not be improvable to become "better designs." Sometimes a good design is good enough, and there isn't much more you can do with it.

You will make LOTS of good designs as a new designer. Over the years, I have made many "good" designs. Those designs worked for their purpose. Most of your designs will be just "good" in your first few years as a designer.

This is important for you to understand because I see many designers paralyzed by wanting their designs to be "best" or "perfect" right from the beginning. This is impossible. Design is a *process; to be a good designer,* we have to get experience.

The four years that we send students to graphic design school is a time for lots of experimentation and building skills. Then the first few years of experience they get from working as a designer right after graduation hones those skills.

Despite what should be an expected trajectory in learning and gaining experience, I meet new designers who expect their designs to be perfect and worthy of printing a month after they learn how to use the pen tool in Illustrator.

Design doesn't work that way. Even with a great eye, design is like any other skill that takes 10,000 hours to master. You must do it consistently, day after day to improve.

Better

I always tell my designers that their goal is to become a little bit better every day. We should not be designing in a vacuum. Instead, we should create enough design work to help us learn what works and what does not.

CB-WT11014 | 6x6 PAPER PAD

Your vacation memories will be as beautiful as the trip that you take in this "Well Traveled" collection. Map out your travel plans with this vintage compilation dedicated to vacations, travel, and getaway destinations. Then pack up and go with the planes, trains, and automobile elements found within this collection. The rich colors and well-worn patterns are sophisticated and timeless. See the world and do it in style!

This collection includes the following:

* Nine double-sided, heavy weight, textured patterned papers
* Three double-sided, heavy weight, textured solid papers
* One 12" X 12" Element Sticker Sheet
* One 12" X 12" Alphabet Sticker Sheet
* Brad Accessory Pack (includes 26 brads)
* 6" x 13" Chipboard Accents
* 5" x 7" Layered Stickers
* Washi Tape
* 4" x 6" Card Pack
* 12" X 12" Collection Kit
* 6" X 6" Paper Pad

CB-WT11013 | 12x12 COLLECTION KIT

CB-WT11019 | PAPRIRUS/OLIVE   CB-WT11020 | CHARCOAL/PARCHMENT

CARTA BELLA

CB-WT11011 | ELEMENT STICKER SHEET

CB-WT11022 | WASHI TAPE

CB-WT11016 | LAYERED STICKERS

4" X 6" CARD EXAMPLES

CARTA BELLA

CB-WT11012 | ALPHA STICKER SHEET   CB-W

CB-WT11002 | FLYING HIGH   CB-WT11003 | ANTIQUE MAP   CB-WT11004 | OLD WORLD DAMASK

CB-WT11005 | THE EXPRESS   CB-WT11006 | WORLD TRAVELER   CB-WT11007 | POSTAGE

CB-WT11008 | TRAVEL CARDS   CB-WT11009 | AIRCRAFT ACE   CB-WT11010 | LET'S GO!

Carina's 2013 Well Traveled Collection for Cartabella

When working on artwork for a manufacturer, the designs need to always be your "best".

"Better" designs graduate from the mediocrity of simply understanding how to use the software. They go to the next level by demonstrating the designer's understanding of how to build an amazing focal point in the design. The design takes the concept of *shape* to the next level so that visually the design *feels* easy yet stimulating. The "better" design builds hierarchy so your eyes can see both everything and the little details dynamically.

Many self-taught designers never make it to this level. They rely on their innate talent and software skills. Many designers find it hard or get stuck between "good" and "better." They aren't sure what could make a design better.

When I was teaching at the University of Minnesota, how to get "better" was solved by simple critique sessions with my students. Having another set of experienced eyes on a design will always help improve it. Sometimes the change to take a design from "good" to "better" was subtle, like tucking a word or letter into an illustration. Sometimes the move from "good" to "better" required a big change, like scrapping an illustration altogether.

There are three reasons most new designers never make it to "better."

1. They do not want to do the work required to improve a design.

2. New skills and design knowledge are necessary to up level the design.

3. They are attached to the design because they put in time, effort, or sentimentality they don't want to lose.

"Better" requires the ability to pivot, let go, and change. It can be as easy or as hard as a designer makes it.

Best

"Best" requires understanding the final purpose of a design. For example, I have been designing quilting cottons for over a decade. When I started, I loved using my designs for apparel for my daughters. Those fabric designs reflected my love for children's apparel by containing many fabrics whose patters were sized for apparel.

Over the years, I became engrossed with quilting. Suddenly, I became much more aware of the colors and sizes of all my designs because they all needed to work together in a quilt. What did my quilt look like when I put a yellow fabric next to a blue one? Was the size different enough between the two to create needed contrast? Experience allowed me to consider questions like these as I created.

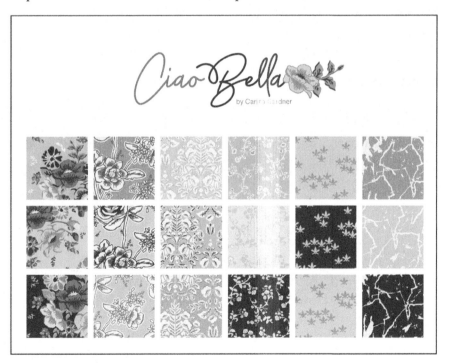

Ciao Bella™ Fabric Collection by Carina Gardner for Riley Blake Designs

When we understand the final purpose of a design, we are more likely to meet the customer's needs. That is why the two defining features of a "best" design are high functionality and customer appropriateness.

This is where experience becomes a key factor. Recently I helped a friend recreate her logo. As a business owner, I use my logos in many ways. I know how a logo will work on a website, on a business card, or on the edge of a fabric collection. Readability is key, and by choosing letters with bigger openings, customers can read the words faster.

A newer designer who is not constantly building logos will take longer to understand what fonts might work best, what the customer wants, or how the logo will be used. The more a designer makes and uses logos, the quicker they will understand the limitations of a design. My experience in logo design helped me to quickly and efficiently deliver a logo to my friend that she ended up loving.

Using the Model

Every designer wants to immediately skip over good and better to get to best. But as I said before, it is a process. Sometimes this process takes time, and sometimes it takes experience. All best designs are the result of effort.

Over the years, I have created thousands of just "good" designs. If you have ever looked me up you will see them. All designers should have lots of "good" designs. Creating thousands of "good" designs is what up levels us. However, you should not stay forever in this stage.

How do you know if you are still in this stage? Here are some qualifying questions:

1. Are you making money from the designs? If the answer is no, it's time to figure out how to become "better."

2. Have your design sales flat-lined? If the answer is yes, it's time to figure out how to become "better."

3. Are you stuck on the same design, reworking it repeatedly? If the answer is yes, it's time to figure out how to become "better."

So how do we move from good to best? Here are a few helpful steps:

1. Analyzing past sales: Which designs sold well and which did not? Is there a way to make those designs better?

2. Experienced eyes: Find a mentor, join a design program, join a group, or go back to college. Get feedback directly on your designs to make them better.

3. Ask yourself the hard questions: Is the design functional? Would you use it in your own home? Have you used it in your own home? Why would anyone else use it? Is it unique enough that there is no competition?

I created an entire Christmas Village with my die-cutting machine a few years ago. I sold it in one of my popular online shops and created educational videos to teach crafters how to make it. The most popular piece in the village was a gingerbread house. It has lots of great details from gumdrops to a frosted snowy roof.

It was one of my "best" designs when I released it.

Fast forward a few years later. I revisited my gingerbread house. I needed to reinvent it. I created an Ultimate Gingerbread house that took me two weeks to design. I felt like an architect trying to figure out the best ways to stabilize it structurally.

When I was finished designing it, I was thrilled! It had 3D evergreen trees, a gazillion little gumdrops, and snowy windows. Using only 12-inch x 12-inch papers, I created an 18-inch W x 14-inch L x 9-inch

D 3D gingerbread house. It was definitely "better" than my previous 'best."

I priced that ultimate gingerbread house more than my original one since it was a more intensive project for advanced crafters. Despite the high price point, I have sold a lot of them because it is a unique piece.

Gingerbread House design for my Christmas Village (to the right) and the Ultimate Gingerbread houses done on a 12 inch Silhouette Cameo and a 24 inch Silhouette Pro (below)

Fast forward a couple more years and the die-cutting company I worked for came out with a machine that cut 24-inch x 24-inch papers. Now I felt like I could test the structure of the design. I cut the entire thing out to create a monstrously huge gingerbread house bigger than my ten-year-old.

Note: *This particular gingerbread house was extremely popular on my @carinagardner Instagram feed if you want to see me build it.*

The point of this story is that "best" changes according to where you are as a designer. As I constantly try to outdo my own designs, reinvent, or showcase them in a new way, a design can become "best" repeatedly. This happens when you are aware of your best sellers and ask, "And now what?" to see if you can exploit your design work to the fullest potential.

You can also see that what was your "best" two years ago might be outdone by a project you are working on now. So the Good Better Best Model works on a sliding scale. What was your "best" yesterday, might be your "better" now because you worked out how to make your design even better.

Your goal is always to be creating your "best" stuff. That is how we go from "good" to "better" to "best."

*Carina's 2021 Ava Kate Collection for
Riley Blake Designs*

# CHAPTER 5
BEING A DESIGN DETECTIVE

U ncovering the truth about our design work need not be filled with drama. If you look at it through the lens of a good mystery—with you as the lead detective—then you will be surprised at how you are your own best Sherlock Holmes!

Like Sherlock Holmes, you must allow yourself the space to detach emotionally from your designs so that you can evaluate them logically. Here are the core questions I ask myself when I am designing.

1. How is a customer going to use this design?

2. Is the design work good enough or different enough?

3. Is the artwork good, better, or best?

Let's take a deep dive into each of these questions.

How is a customer going to use this design?

I enjoy creating dingbats. A dingbat is simply a font that uses illustrations, not alphabet letters, for all the keys. I went through a serious dingbat phase for a couple of years because they were just so darn easy for me to design.

However, when I looked at the sales, I noticed a pattern. Some of my lined illustrations didn't perform as well as my filled illustrations. I was selling these mainly in my Silhouette shop, where people were buying designs to cut on their machines. I had assumed that customers knew how to use the designs. I explored whether this assumption was wrong.

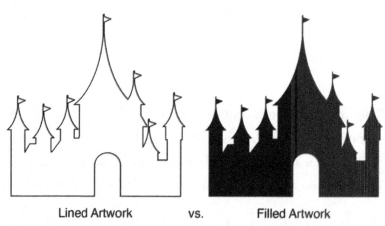

Lined Artwork   vs.   **Filled Artwork**

Since these were sold in one of my stores where crafters wanted die-cut shapes, the lined images were harder to visualize for a die-cut machine. I knew they could be cut, but I rarely showed examples of how they could be used.

Customers didn't understand how to use the lined dingbat designs.

Upon that realization, I created a series of four dingbat videos for my YouTube channel (youtube.com/carinagardner), teaching people how to cut the lined dingbats and how there were *more* possibilities with lined illustrations. I included an instruction tutorial on my dingbat products that took them straight to an educational video. I also included mock-ups of some of my illustrations on mugs and cards so they could see better how to utilize the designs.

I easily could have doubted my design work or gone down a "poor me" rabbit hole upon realizing some of my designs were not selling.

But instead of embracing the drama, I stepped back and asked the question, "How is a customer going to use this design?" I knew how they could use it but it became clear that I wasn't *educating* my customers on how to use it.

So instead of being upset no one was buying those designs, I got to work and created videos and tutorials that taught crafters how to use them.

How often do you second guess your design work instead of being a detective? You will be surprised at what you can uncover if you look carefully at the circumstances.

Is the design work good enough or different enough?

I am relatively objective with my work. It's what made me a good Creative Director. Being objective allows me to rework or throw away designs that do not work. This is because I am unattached to my designs. I know when something is my best work and when I can improve it. But I also know when to stop and leave it at "good" or "better."

If a design is just "good," often it is not "good enough" or different enough to compete. As designers, we need to create work that is different or functional to cut through the sea of designs.

A good example is the unicorn face motif that became popular a few years ago. If you have not seen this illustration, it is a flat unicorn horn, eyes, and a nose, sometimes with flowers or other illustrations to make it special.

I came late to the trend, and I knew it. I submitted a few designs long after it was popular on a week when I was feeling uninspired.

Did they do well? No.

Was I sad or surprised by the results? Also no.

See, we can't be surprised when we build designs that are already out there and trending. The first person who created that design benefited from the trend. Everyone else was late to the game.

Early in my design business, I built an incredibly simple set of film frames. A video I created taught scrapbookers how to use these film frames in an album I made to go along with them. I was surprised when crafters bought these like crazy. The design rose to the top of the trending list.

One week later, several other designers who had seen those frames do well made similar frames hoping to copy the trend. And although my design stayed at the top, I would be lying if I said I didn't feel frustrated so many people had copied me.

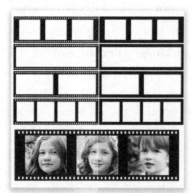

Photo Filmstrips from the Travel Stories Die Cut Set

I tell you this story to illustrate a couple of different points. First, I did well off the design because I was the creator. I was the first to implement and educate using that design. I also made the most money from that design because I was ahead of the copycats. I was creating the trend.

Second, copying is a real thing that gets designers down. But instead of letting it get me down, I used being ahead of everyone else on the trend to create a lot of other designs so I could *stay* ahead. Are you the designer in everyone else's shadow or are you trying to build your own special trends?

Spending your whole career worrying about everyone copying you is not helpful. Instead, create from a place of abundance and don't look too hard at those in your shadow. Instead, move ahead designing in full confidence that you have something special and creative to share. Make yourself the trendsetter.

Is the artwork good, better, or best?

Part of being a great detective about our work is knowing when our work is just good, is something better, or is our very best. This requires self-awareness, experience, and being okay with the truth. It also requires us to do a little research.

I like being a designer because I get a lot of energy from being alone. I like the quiet and creativity of my design work. This little island I am on helps me focus and create. While it is one of my strengths, it is also my biggest weakness.

One of the problems with being alone is that I am not always assessing outside trends or discovering just *how good* the competition out there is.

Let me give you an example. My daughter is working on an animation degree. During her first semester of college, she was exposed to the peer-grading system many professors employ to help students understand how their artwork ranks.

In her case, the professor laid out on the board three categories. The "okay" area, the "middle" area, and the "best" area. All the student art work was mixed up and passed around to the students to assess. As a group they had to equally distribute the artwork between the three categories. Everyone's artwork couldn't go into "best."

Students placed artwork on the board and moved it around based on how good they thought the artwork was compared to everything that was in the room.

You can imagine how mortifying it would be to be in the bottom third of the class and how elated you would be if you were in the top third. It is a tough exercise, but a revealing one.

From my experience as a university instructor, when an art or design student asks why they didn't get an "A" on a project, it's because they didn't see all the other projects in the room. By seeing what is out there, you better understand where you stand as a designer. This is not to make you feel less than (it will only make you feel less than if you take it personally, which is why you need to think of your design work objectively). Instead, objectively comparing yourself to the rest of the market helps you become a better designer. Rise to the level already out there and then rise *above* it. But this is only possible if you can go out and objectively assess the current design climate.

This is tough to do since I see many of my designers fall into the trap of comparison when they do this. If you are vulnerable to this or impostor syndrome then do not do this research often. Instead, set a timer and do the research from a social media platform or search engine that does not trigger a negative response. This is not perusing the Internet for the fun of it. This is researching what designs are doing well and what customers want. It is a different experience when you go into the process as a researcher instead of as an observer.

I can always tell when a new designer has not done their research. Several designers have shown me their portfolio and are confused when a fabric or paper manufacturer has not picked them up. Sometimes I hear the phrase, "But this is as good as other things I've seen out there!" To this I respond, "But is it better? Original? Unique? Because if it is not, you will not get a contract." Why would a manufacturer contract with a designer making artwork just as good as the designers they already have? Manufacturers are interested in designers with something special and unique to add to their current products.

Your goal is not to make what is already selling out there but to make something that stands out in the crowd. It doesn't mean you go out and make something crazy and different (although sometimes that works). It usually means that you make something just different enough in a new marketplace and new format so that it is accepted as something unique.

A good example of this is my gingerbread house. I'm sure I wasn't the first to design a gingerbread house out of paper. I designed the gingerbread house in my style. Then I took it to the next level by seeing how big I could make it. It was unique because I added scale to my own particular style…not because I had invented gingerbread houses.

Become a design detective. Understand your own style and what hurdles are specific to your business. Use the Problem Solving Cycle to reveal possibilities. Dig into your designs and ask yourself why things are not selling. Leave the emotions around why it is not selling behind therefore getting rid of the drama. Learn how to create "best" designs and outdo yourself to help make your work stand out. Be in front of the trends by being a trendsetter yourself but also by being aware of current trends through regular research into the industry.

Beware comparison. Instead, logically find solutions and styles that work for you.

Creating the artwork and digitizing it is part of
Phase 2 of the Design Process: Implementation

CHAPTER 6
THE DESIGN PROCESS

When I started my first digital scrapbooking shop, which essentially launched me into owning a business, my main goal was to design as much as I could.. Every day I churned out 6 patterned papers and packaged them into a digital preview. I would place that preview on my website with an "add to cart" button.

Below are the essential first operational steps of creating a design business.

Even as my business has become more complicated, doing these main four activities is how a design business grows.

Here's the simple version of it. I had an idea for a product. I designed the product. I packaged the product. I asked for sales.

I would tell a new designer that these actions should be the core of their new venture.

My Design Process Model is one that I have used as the foundation of my business from the beginning.

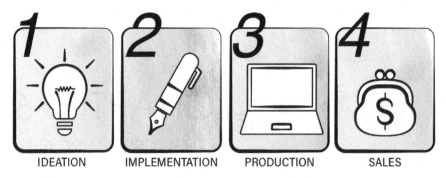

| IDEATION | IMPLEMENTATION | PRODUCTION | SALES |

The Design Process Model™

I will bet that as you look at this model, you will be able to tell which areas you excel at and which you are ignoring. That's why it is so powerful. Because if you know what you are NOT doing, you can make real changes.

Ideation

I rarely have to talk to designers about ideation. New designers are excited for all the possibilities. They want to design fabric, papers, die cuts, printables, journals, and everything else under the sun. The world is a new designer's oyster!

If you are brimming full of new ideas all the time then design is a great place for you because you will always be excited for the next project. Having lots of ideas will push you to become a better designer as you implement them all.

Implementation

Up to this point, I have focused on the "design" of your design business. This is the "Implementation" piece of the model. Designing a product should be the foundation of everything you do.

Implementation is where you will apply the "Good Better Best" model. It will allow you to build a foundation as a great designer.

I cannot recommend enough for those who are self-taught to improve your software skills and design knowledge. Working towards becoming the best at what you do is the key to becoming successful and the implementation phase is where much of this growth occurs.

Your designs are the products of your business. As you implement and take action, your skills as an implementor will flourish.

Production

For years, I disliked production. I found it tedious. In the past few years, however, I have found it to be my favorite part of the process because it is relaxing after a day of designing.

Production is simply preparing a product for market. This looks different depending on who the customer is. If you are preparing a design for a manufacturer, you might check the spot colors and color mode. If you are creating a digital product, this might be your digital kit preview and your zip files.

Production consists of a project's detailed final checklist to ensure that it is ready for a customer to use.

You can see why I did not love these tasks for many years. After implementing great design work, it wasn't fun going through each document and ensuring it had the correct bleeds, UPC codes, and more.

After a few years, I realized that I had gotten good at production and that it was a great way to rest my brain. Instead of using a lot of creative and mental energy designing, I would turn on a movie or podcast and use production time as "downtime" after a long work day.

I came to rely on this production time to rejuvenate me at the end of a long day of designing.

Sales

Once you have a beautiful and functionally-designed product, you are ready to move into sales.

For me, the word "business" is not scary. It sounds downright cool. What I did not realize when I started my design business was that "business" is just another word for *sales*.

If you shudder at the word *sales*, you are not the only one. The word *sales* brings up a lot of complicated feelings in designers. We know we should do "sales" but it feels icky. As artists and designers, we sometimes feel that others should not have to pay for the beauty we have created. We might worry that others will see us as the greasy car salesman. Or maybe we aren't sure that our artwork is worth selling, so we fear being vulnerable.

These reasons are why many designers spend their time only on ideation and implementation. Ideation and implementation are the design aspects, while production and sales are the business aspects.

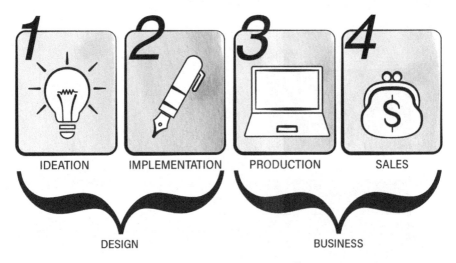

The Design Process Model™

I have run into hundreds, if not thousands, of designers who tell me they have a design business. When I ask them what they sell, they tell me all about the products they create. Sometimes it's stationery, cards, or clip art. Sometimes they have created many seamless patterns or papers.

But the more I inquire and learn the details, the more they admit that they have sold little or nothing. They tell me they are "just getting started." Upon deeper conversation, I'll discover that "getting started" has taken them two years or more.

The danger any designer who is "getting started" faces is falling into the trap of thinking that by simply designing, they have a design business. Having a design business is not something we are taught in school. We are instead taught to *follow our passion. Create beautiful things. Fill the world with our unique style.*

While these are all true and necessary elements to having a design business, just doing these things does not create a *business*. Just because we have had a product idea, implemented it, and maybe even produced it, does not mean that we have a business.

*Examples of Production from
Carina's 2013 Dishware &
Towel Collection for Deseret Book*

Testing files is a part of the Production Phase

We do not have a business until we have *sales*.

Like you, it was hard for me to come to terms with what sales looked like. That's why I had stayed on my own website for the first eleven months. It was a *safe place to sell.*

What resulted from selling on only my own site? Very litter in terms of sales.

I found that to make the word "sales" more palatable to my designer sensibilities, I had to stop thinking about what was safe and think about what was practical. I even had to realize that "sales" was happening at levels that I had not considered before.

For example, when I started talks with Echo Park Paper Co. about creating Cartabella with them, I was actually engaged in "sales" because I was selling them on the idea of the new company: I had the designers and connections to produce all the creativity that a new scrapbooking company would need. Echo Park, too, was engaged in "sales" because they were selling me on their ability to fulfill, lead, and distribute the product. What was happening was ALL SALES, but it didn't feel that way. I was trying to determine if they were a good fit for me as a Creative Director, and they were trying to determine if I was a good fit for them.

This was sales. Because I went into it not with the idea that getting "salesy" is scary, but instead trying to discover logically if they were a good fit for my skills and vice versa; all the "sales" was just conversation.

Remember when I moved from my own website onto a new website and suddenly saw success? That was because I was making good *sales* decisions, not implementation decisions. I chose a shop that sold my product for a percentage of my price. They provided the audience. First, I had to *sell* them on the idea that I was a good fit for their shop

CB-SN13014 | 6x6 PAPER PAD

Taken from the pages of your favorite books, the "So Noted" collection is rich in Regency period imagery, including silhouettes, musical notes, and vintage lace. Patterns include a modern twist with a soft color scheme. Become the author of your own story! Capture your thoughts, your memories, and your dreams while journaling on the pages of this notable collection.

This collection includes the following:

* Nine double-sided, heavy weight, textured patterned papers
* Three double-sided, heavy weight, textured solid papers
* One 12" X 12" Element Sticker Sheet

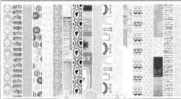

CB-SN13013 | 12x12 COLLECTI

CB-SN13002 | ALWAYS YOU   CB-SN13003 | TINY LACE   CB-SN13004 | SCRIPT & SCRIBBLES

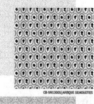

CB-SN13005 | ANTIQUE SILHOUETTES   CB-SN13006 | DEAR JANE   CB-SN13007 | MUSICAL SCORE

CB-SN13008 | NOTE CARDS   CB-SN13009 | VINTAGE FRAMES   CB-SN13010 | INKED NUMERALS

INTRODUCING SO NOTED SOLIDS

CB-SN13018 | PORCELAIN BLUE/VINTAGE GREEN   CB-SN13019 | CITRON/PALE PINK   CB-SN13020 | PRISTINE PRINT/EGGSHELL BLUE

INTRODUCING 4" X 6" CARDS

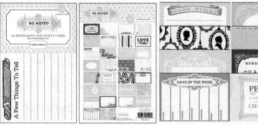

CB-SN12021 | 4" X 6" CARDS   4" X 6" CARD EXAMPLES

CARTA BELLA

Creation of the papers is part of the Implementation Phase. Creating the catalog is Production & Sales

(via an application). Next, I had to *sell* my designs to their customers by simply putting up many products for them to purchase every week. Then I *sold* them further by showing them what they could do with my products on my YouTube channel.

Sales in the design industry is simply finding the right audience for your product and then executing on the creation of product to fit the audience and then educating the audience on how to use that product.

As designers, we have a much easier job than many other businesses in finding those audiences. If you are a die-cut designer, find shops where die cuts are being sold. If you are a fabric designer, find manufacturers or shops where fabric is being sold.

It is as simple as that.

How to Use The Design Process Model

Every piece of this model is essential; each can become more complex as you delve into it. For example, as you create product ideas, you will want to organize them into categories. I like figuring out if an idea is useful now or if I need to park it for another time.

Implementation of your designs will require you to hone your design skills. You will need to create both beautiful and functional pieces for your business.

Great production will help you avoid customer service issues.

Finally, sales will help determine your current skill set's best audiences, shops, and manufacturers. And by the way, whether you are making good, better, or best designs, there IS a place for your designs. The Internet allows you to test your skills at all levels, which is why I can teach even new designers to make money in starter shops online.

Match your skill to an online shop, freelance job, or manufacturer and watch sales come in. You will see that as you improve and design more products, your sales will also increase. This correlation has been proven repeatedly by my designers.

As you might have guessed, all designers find themselves comfortably in Ideation and Implementation. Most never get to Production and Sales. Here is the ironic thing about this sad cycle. Those who make it to production and sales become BETTER at Ideation and Implementation. Those that stay in the safety of Ideation and Implementation struggle to become better designers.

This is because the sales process actually forces a designer to become better. They see what manufacturers and online shops like, and they then push their artwork to that standard.

By stretching ourselves for customers and companies, designers progress to those new levels of better and best. There is no compelling reason to stretch ourselves when we design only for ourselves. When we are never critiqued for our work, whether in an educational program, by a creative director, or even by our customers via sales, then why would we bother to improve?

Fully using the Design Process Model is a challenge and an uphill climb that makes us better designers.

Identifying the Holes In Your Design Process

Every designer has a different stumbling block in their design process. Some get stuck in ideation. Others love spending time on production. Many never get around to real sales.

The medium you are working in often will also determine where you need to spend your time as a designer.

For example, a new designer might tell me they applied to be a fabric designer and that they were rejected. The problem for that designer is likely implementation.

Fabric contracts require such a high level of design work that the implementation needs to be high level to get a contract. You need to be doing your "best" work to get that contract.

How about a designer who has an online shop without making any sales. Sitting down and looking on their computer reveals fifty products that need uploading. In this case, the problem is clearly sales. This designer isn't finishing the full design process and is stuck by their own procrastination.

It is not complicated to discover where the hole is in your design process. You can always do a time study on your activities to determine if you are spending enough time on the correct activities.

Note: You can do a time study exercise as outlined in the free workbook at: www.designprofitprosperbook.com.

Wherever you are stuck, using the Design Process Model to evaluate your work can help you figure out how to improve your workflow. It is an easy way to evaluate what you are doing right and wrong in your business.

Carina's 2016 Posy Gardner Collection for Riley Blake Designs in her Simply Modern Patchwork Quilts eBook with her son Charlie

CHAPTER 7
THE THREE HURDLES

In high school, I tried out for the track team. I spent one season on the cross country team and decided that I liked running enough to try out for hurdling.

But being a good runner doesn't mean you will be a good jumper. On my first day on the track, I tried to jump the track hurdles. The coaches showed me the technique, how to run, and when to jump. I practiced without the hurdle and finally gained the confidence to jump a single hurdle.

Imagine my surprise at the sudden rush of fear I felt when approaching the hurdle. I suddenly felt strongly that I could not jump over it. It looked way too tall for me. I slammed on my running brakes right before I jumped and ran right into the hurdle.

The other runners assured me it was okay to feel afraid and to try again.

So I did. But several times, I came to the hurdle and stopped.

After several attempts, I finally found the courage to jump. When I jumped, I did not get enough air between myself and the hurdle and one of my feet hooked the hurdle and CRASH, we both came down.

Now if I thought I was scared *before*, this felt like a major setback. Now I had the scrapes on my knees as prove that I couldn't jump high enough.

Fortunately, I like to compete with myself. Even though I had fallen, I now understood how high I needed to jump to make it over that hurdle. So although I feared falling, I tried again.

The second time, I grazed the hurdle, and my balance was off, so I went down again. More blood. More scrapes. But this time, I felt like I knew how high I needed to jump.

So the third time, I jumped, and I didn't touch the hurdle. I was thrilled!

As I kept practicing, sometimes I wouldn't get enough air and would hit the hurdles and fall. Other times I would get enough air for the first hurdle, but then fall down at the second hurdle.

Hurdle jumping is similar to the hurdles we face when creating a design business.

Certain barriers keep us from going through the "Good, Better, Best" Model and the "Design Process" Model. When we come upon these hurdles, there is a surge of fear about whether we are going to be able to jump over them.

Like me, you might have stopped right before one of these design hurdles because fear seizes you. You might have thought, "Who am I to be trying to do this?" or "This looks way too hard to learn at my age."

Maybe you are someone who got enough air to jump over hurdle one but can't seem to get over hurdle two. With practice and perseverance, we can jump all the hurdles necessary to create a design business.

It's important to acknowledge these hurdles also as milestones in your business. Seeing them for what they are and how important they are to help you stand out will bring credibility to your business.

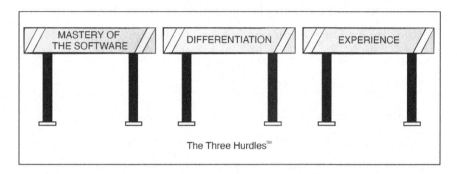

The Three Hurdles™

Hurdle 1: Mastery of the Software

There is a direct correlation between Hurdle 1 "Mastery of the Software" and Level 1 "Good" of the Good Better Best Model. Believe it or not, designers should be grateful for this first hurdle. Those that will put in the hard work to learn the technology have the upper hand.

This barrier to entry works to everyone's advantage. When I have aspiring designers fight me on learning Illustrator, I usually just let them do what they want. If they cannot be convinced that a vector-based software is necessary to have a full design business, I'll let them see how far they can jump without it.

Mastery of the software isn't about one software. It is knowing how to use multiple softwares together so that you get the best results from your efforts. This means vector and pixel-based programs or even font programs. It might also mean knowing how to use different tools or devices.

Hurdle 1 "Mastery of the Software" simply means a designer is willing to learn and relearn software that will get them the desired result. This means they have to exhibit grit and adaptability.

Hurdle 2: Differentiation

When working with my designers, the first year is spent learning the software and becoming good at general design work. There does come a point when a designer must show that they are skilled or different in the marketplace.

There are lots of different ways to do this. Perhaps it is creating a specialized product. It might be the volume of products the designer makes. Maybe it is a style or defining look so different from anything else.

No matter what it is, differentiation is how designers start making money. As a designer for a company, your job would be to create products that look right for that company, right? The same is true for a design business. Create things that make you different from every other designer so that your work stands out.

Hurdle 2 correlates strongly with "better" in the Good Better Best model because once you succeed at learning the technology, you can dive deeper into becoming a strong designer. This is because you are no longer fighting the software. You can use the software to your advantage by understanding technology's limits.

Hurdle 3: Experience

There are no shortcuts to becoming a professional designer. Use your time to create experiences that teach you to be a proficient designer.

A few years back, I started a kids paper company. I understood how to make a product but I clearly did not understand how to distribute the product. My experience was to go to a trade show and sell the product to stores. Unfortunately, I didn't understand the childrens and baby market as well as I did the scrapbooking market so I missed the mark for merchandising. It took me a couple of trade shows to figure out how to sell the product in a way that was useful to stores.

That is only one example of many things I learned about the physical product industry when I owned that company. I also learned how to contract designers, how independent toy sellers worked, how big box chains differed, and how to sell in that industry. Some of that information is transferable into other industries. Some of it is not. All of it was important to gain experience I have today.

Building experience as a designer will make you a better fit for the industry you are designing for and the manufacturers you work for. This is a time-driven tool. The more clients, freelance, online shops, and manufacturers you work for, the more you will have the confidence to make decisions for your design business.

Throughout this book, I have shown you pictures from projects from over the years. Some of those designs are more successful than others. I am grateful for all those experiences because the journey has made me the designer I am today. Delight in the day to day journey as a designer because it will help you jump the biggest hurdle of all: experience.

How to Deal With the Hurdles

These three hurdles show up over and over again for my designers because they usually come in this order (1. Software, 2. Differentiation, and 3. Experience), however I have noticed that designers who are willing to do these things almost simultaneously have a faster, more profitable experience than others.

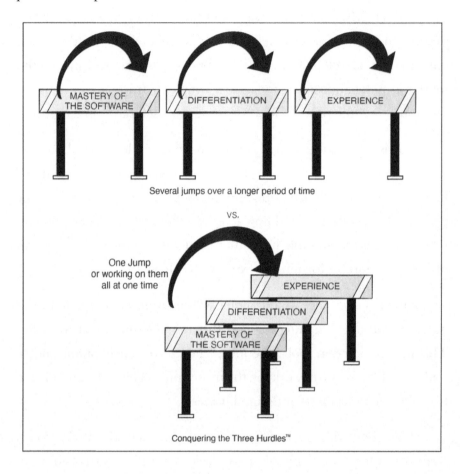

Conquering the Three Hurdles™

Let me break it down further. I learned the software while in college. Sometimes I was learning it right before I was teaching it since the software was so new. However, Differentiation and Experience were happening almost at the same time when I started my business.

What I wondered was whether the Mastery of Software Hurdle could be jumped at the same time as the Differentiation and Experience hurdles. Could a brand new designer also learn how to make sales as they were learning the tools?

This was something I tested in my Design Suite program and determined that not only could designers learn and sell as they go, they become more profitable *sooner* than their counterparts who go to online courses or college.

As indicated in the example of the hurdles above, the hardest part is that a single big jump takes more momentum and courage than doing three smaller jumps. Ironically, I find that most self taught designers are in fact doing the single jump by themselves. So when they jump, fall, and are discouraged, it's not surprising that they do not want to get back up and try again.

I believe that you can jump hurdles all at the same time. But just like with jumping the hurdles separately, designers have to expect that the process of learning the software, differentiation, and gaining experience will take more time than they expect. That being said, taking the time to jump the hurdles is worth the effort in the end because doing so will unlock your money-making potential.

From Carina's 2017 Sweetly Stitched Quilts eBook
and favorite project posted to social media often.

CHAPTER 8
THE CONUNDRUM OF SOCIAL MEDIA

When I started designing, social media was not really a thing. Over the past few years, it has changed the landscape for personal brands.

But it has also muddied the waters for new designers to understand marketing and sales.

Social media often feels like a safe sales fix for designers. However, do not confuse branding for sales. New designers feel they are creating *sales* by posting to social media. However, for most companies, social media is used more as a public relations tool than a sales vehicle. Often new designers plunge into their new careers, believing that social media should be a major part of their business activities. This is untrue, and here is why.

What social media actually does for your business

Your audience numbers will be low when you start on any social media platform. This is because you are getting started, so that's okay! Because they will be low, you will have very few eyeballs on your posts. The algorithm will make it difficult for the people following you to see your posts since you compete with all the other feeds.

If you would like evidence for why you should not use social media as your sales vehicle when you start your design business, then join me in the following thought exercise

Ponder on your own social media habits for a moment. First, how often have you purchased directly from a social media platform? Next, how often do you engage in posts from the companies or people you purchase from?

I purchase from social media probably twice a month. Considering I follow thousands of people and companies, only a very small percentage of who I follow are actually making money from me. Furthermore, when I look at my purchasing track record, it is almost exclusively from ads of companies I have already done business with.

Do you do the same thing? Maybe sometimes you will shop from a company you haven't purchased from before, but I suspect it is a rare occurrence.

Initially, when trying to learn how to design and create products, the only thing social media will do for you is help you build a brand. Building a brand is important but it is not the most important thing during your business's first months and years.

The myth

New designers believe they must build a reliable social media brand to get sales.

This is a myth.

Thank goodness it is a myth. Because the odds are completely against you on social media…especially in the first few years.

Designers are designers, NOT influencers.

I know plenty of designers who don't use social media. Many are making a lot of money with no online presence. Yet, somehow there is a persistent belief that to be a business, you must have a social media presence.

What is the difference between an influencer and a designer? When you are an influencer, you will build an audience by entertaining and educating them. Influencers give away free content and downloads on their website or platform to keep engagement high. This is their full-time job.

After years of garnering people's attention and trust, the influencer will make money from sponsorships and brand deals. It is a difficult road that takes time and strategy.

Designers make money from their *designs*. Like increasing the amount of content they post can help an influencer level up, the number of products will help a designer level up.

Unfortunately, the lines have become blurred over the years. New designers see seasoned designers with followings and assume that it is because of their following they make money when the opposite is true. A good designer gets a dedicated following after years of creating great products.

The exception to the rule

There are exceptions to this rule. In particular, in the quilting cottons world, sometimes new designers are picked up because they have a massive social media presence. Manufacturers use that to help grow their audiences. Some design their own lines. Others use clip art. Some don't design their collections at all! The manufacturer's team designs their lines.

If you are reading this book, I hope your goal is to become a full-fledged designer, not one of these designers. You can learn more about this in the free workbook, available at www.designprofitprosperbook.com.

Your new strategy

If you have plans to incorporate social media into your design business, stop to rethink this for a moment. During a 40-hour week, if a designer spends 25 hours in designing/implementation, ten in production, and five on sales, what time is there for branding and marketing? If those five sales hours are spent on social media, and you are not getting sales, is it any wonder that you feel like you are failing? You are competing with influencers who spend more than five hours a week creating content. You also aren't using those five sales hours for meaningful sales activities.

Creating content for social media dips into design or production time, which is vital time for new designers. Think of it as the vitamins and minerals a body needs as it grows. Designers need that design time to become great designers. I try to steer my new designers clear of social media.

Now imagine if all the time spent on social media were spent instead on designing. Let's say two new designers are starting businesses. Designer A spends an extra five hours a week designing. Designer B spends those same hours creating content for social media. Designer B will have a few hundred followers at the end of a year if they are lucky and have no sales.

However, Designer A will have 260 more design hours than Designer B. If they are using the sales strategy I outline in Chapter 9 instead of social media, then they will also be on their way to making sales in year two. The designer who has more design time will be a far *better designer* than Designer B.

Part of how we make our mark as a designer is by being a better designer (refer back to the Good, Better, Best Model). Think back to the example of the college class where everyone divides the work up into three groups. Your goal is to make it into the top third of the class, not the middle.

Let's be clear, I am not opposed to social media. I think it is an important part of your overall long-term business strategy. Some of you might have even found this book because of social media! It is just rarely relevant in the *first year* of your design business. The early years of your design business, especially if you did not get formal schooling, should concentrate on designing product. It will put you ahead of the competition in a few important ways.

First, the more time you spend designing, the more products you will create. Designer A will have a significantly larger number of finished products to sell than Designer B simply because they put in so many more hours.

Second, because Designer A has put in more time designing, they will bridge the gap between good and better faster than Designer B. Remember that this is the only way we can make our mark as designers. We must produce beautiful and high functioning products that are different in the marketplace.

Third, Designer A will become faster in the software than Designer B. By spending that much time early in the business on designing, the software will become easier and easier to use, making that designer faster. A faster designer creates *more output*, which means more to sell.

Finally, by the time year one ends, if Designer A starts posting on social media, they will easily catch up to Designer B because they already have many products to showcase. They will also have some sense of their style. The first year there is more experimentation; sometimes, social media makes a designer feel like they cannot change styles or products. Mitigate that by simply not posting in year one.

When to break this rule

There will always be the person who becomes a designer after they already have a social media following or who feels that they want to break the above rule for their own reasons. If you MUST break this rule, here are a few guidelines.

1. If you already have a following, continue with the content you were already posting but thank about diminishing the time you spend on building content so that you have more design time. The goal isn't to NOT use social media. The goal is to get in more design time.

2. If you feel you must post to social media, keep it simple. Post pictures of products you are selling. Or videos that take only five minutes to make.

3. If you create educational content for your products, social media becomes customer service! This is different from using it for sales. Instead, it is a way to build relationships.

A little more on #3.

Most of my design business's early years were spent building "how to" blog posts and videos. The goal was to teach people how to use my products and to decrease the number of emails I would receive from confused customers.

This became especially necessary as my products became more complex or had more pieces. Building educational written or video content is *always* a good business practice. It will save you time eventually and teach your customers that the products you create are reliable.

If you are creating this content then add this information to your platforms. However, generally, new designers aren't ready to create these complex designs. Products designed by new designers are usually straightforward for customers to understand. This is why there is rarely a time when #3 occurs in the first year. I see #3 being used more and more by designers in my program, but that is simply because they are in a fast-paced process of building their design business.

The goal of social media

After the initial year or even the first few years, social media can be a helpful tool. Use it for brand management and educational content. It is a great way to help customers trust and like you.

Finally, you can use social media to sell and create an audience once you are fast and efficient in the software programs, have a unique viewpoint, and have the time available to devote to it. Social media CAN be a source of sales but will more likely help you build your brand.

CHAPTER 9
SALE MAGIC

I wish I could tell you that I was that entrepreneurial kid that opened the lemonade stand or started a bake sale to make some extra money. But I don't remember doing any of that.

I was actually the kid that hid in her closet playing make-believe, sewing doll clothes, and writing imaginative plays.

I know a lot of designers who are the same, so selling a product to a customer seems downright intimidating. Luckily, sales for designers can be an easy process. Some of these methods for making money are downright magical for introverted artist types.

While there are more ways to make money than I have mentioned here, I love these methods because they feel natural and easy. Choose the ones that work with your personality and interests.

Freelance Design

One of the earliest sales strategies I got involved with was freelance design work. Most of my projects came by word of mouth. While I was working on my Ph.D. I even scored logo work for an online agency. It was my first time working for a company I only dealt with over the Internet.

One of my first projects was from a woman at church who heard I was a designer. She wanted labels for a new line of natural soaps that she was creating. Another contact needed someone to create a logo and website images for a company that they were working for. News spread I was working on a Masters and Ph.D. in Design, and projects rolled in.

Freelance is a natural way to create design income because it generally happens because somebody knows somebody who knows somebody. People *need* design services and you know the software to provide them. It's an easy exchange of time for money.

Several designers I work with now may be building an online shop or working for a company but still take side jobs doing custom wallpaper orders, logos, stationery, and so much more.

The key to easy freelancing is creating a network of people who know what you do for a living. That means not shying away from telling people you are a designer at a party. It means embracing the title so your confidence shines through. Often the person you are talking to may not need a designer, but someone they know does. It's like six degrees of Kevin Bacon, although it's only one or two degrees away. New small businesses *need* freelance designers. You solve their problem.

To fill up your schedule with freelance work, several agencies and websites now exist for freelancers. It is a matter of finding the right one for you. Long gone are the days where if you did not have a network, you would get no work.

The main three things you need to start a freelance business are

1. A portfolio

2. A flexible design style

3. The ability to discern the needs of customers

I occasionally will take a side freelance job but most of the freelance work that comes to me now goes to the designers in my program. I love that freelance stretches my designers in ways they never expected to be stretched. It makes them far superior designers and gives them more of Hurdle #3 Experience.

Online Shops

My absolute favorite way to make money as a designer is through online shops. Every online shop has different application processes and rules, but they are a great way to create reliable monthly income.

I have thrived off of online shops for over fifteen years. They have been the core of my design business and I can confidently recommend them to designers.

When I started as a designer, online shops were new and unreliable. Shops would come and go based on the profitability of the owners.

Now most shops are owned and managed by bigger entities making the income and audiences much more reliable. This is a huge plus for designers willing to put time into building a large volume of products in one shop.

Online shops have also become much savvier with their application and upload processes. Many have easy-to-use portals to upload designs, add descriptions, and even keywords. As someone who lived through the process and has been in multiple shops, let me tell you that it has never been easier to become a digital designer!

Part of the reason I greatly love online shops is that there is no entry barrier. My early work was "good," but still got accepted. This allowed me to get "better" and "best" because I was consistently uploading to those online shops. It is what made creating income while developing a style possible.

Online shop design work does two very important things.

1. You can learn and develop a style while still making money.

2. You can easily pivot as you do market research in the niche you are designing for.

I find that selling through an online shop allows a designer to see what they can accomplish. It also helps refine a designer for contracts and freelance work.

For many aspiring designers going back to college is not a great option. Instead, if you use the first four years of your design business as the "great design experiment" you will be far ahead of those that go back to college. Why? Because you are mashing all the hurdles together and jumping them simultaneously.

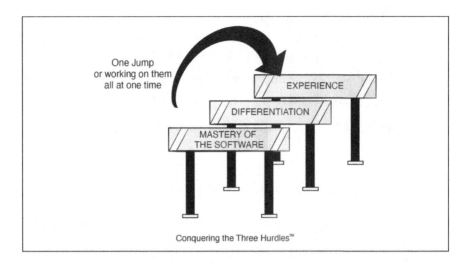

Conquering the Three Hurdles™

Because of this, designers might feel that the jump is too big or too hard. It is a lot of working on software, differentiation, and experience simultaneously, which is why doing it this way is not for the faint of heart. If you need to spread it out, you can by working on the three hurdles individually for years at a time. However, I believe you will get faster results if you work on all three things at once.

Let me explain a little more about this. You must learn the software when you first start as a designer. As you learn the software, you will make little illustrations or projects. You could stop there and slowly accomplish overcoming Hurdle #1. However, if instead you put those projects up and sell them on an online shop, you can then start working on Hurdle #2 Differentiation and Hurdle #3 Experience.

Differentiation requires many products to hone down a style. Experience requires time and analyzing results. By taking the extra step of testing your products in the marketplace after learning the software, you will eventually get both differentiation and experience.

The crazy thing is that by following these steps, you will get closer to your "best" work, which is what every designer should strive for.

Choosing an Online Shop

I often get asked what shop a designer should join. This is a question I take seriously. The wrong shop will hold a designer back from making progress by six months or a year. Because of this, doing your research is key. Determine if that shop would benefit from your unique style.

1. Find a shop that matches the products you want to create.

2. Determine if that shop would benefit from your unique style.

I sometimes ask whether it is possible to make multiple six figures from online shops. The answer is a resounding yes. Most of the money I have made yearly has come from online sales. I have had shops that made four and five figures every month.

The key to making it financially lucrative for you is discovering how designers win in any shop. That means understanding the strategies that make you make money in any particular shop. It requires you to learn more about the company that runs the shop and how they do business.

Within Design Suite, we built videos on particular online shops so members understand the strategies involved *for that shop*. Every shop is different, like every designer is unique.

Sometimes I will talk to designers and discover that a shop that is financially lucrative for one is terrible for another. It is all about how you utilize the policies of the selling market.

Here are my recommended strategy questions you should ask yourself once you have chosen a shop:

1. What are the actions and behaviors of the designers in this shop?

2. How many products do these designers produce weekly or monthly?

3. What makes my design work special or unique so I can stand out?

4. How can I help educate customers more about my products in this shop?

5. How do I communicate with the shop owner or creative directors so that I do not miss any opportunities?

Your ability to build amazing strategies by simply communicating well with the shop owner and customers is limitless. Understand the behaviors of all who interact with that online shop.

Some of the bigger online shops no longer have a process for communicating with the shop owner. A large corporation may own it and their goal is simply to have as many products as possible.

In such a case, watching the behaviors of all those involved becomes even more important. Reading and understanding emails that come from that shop is important. Knowing how many products can be uploaded daily and what categories are most popular will help you determine what to make. Develop strategies for how you can stand out.

As a designer, you are building visual solutions. As a design business owner, you are developing sales solutions. All it takes is a little critical thinking and patience to build sales practices that will help you build a growing design business.

Other Ways to Make Money

Over the years, I have designed dishware, jewelry, sewing patterns, prints, holiday products, and fabric. Some of these came from companies I had contracts with. Others were products I designed and sold myself.

These are amazing ways to bring in income but they are also more complicated and often require a more sophisticated approach. New designers often want to get a contract quickly with a manufacturer because they are so excited to see their products in real life.

While pitching a company and getting a contract is not impossible, it is very difficult. Most companies find it more economical to hire in-house designers, so they do not need contract designers. For minimalist, modern, or clean-lined designers, these contracts are more difficult to get than other styles because these are designs that an in-house designer can easily imitate.

So if getting a licensed deal is your cup of tea, here are a few things to think about before the pitch:

1. Are your designs seasoned enough to be worth considering by a creative director?

2. Is your style unique and difficult to imitate, making you more valuable?

3. Do you bring your own audience and community with you from social media and other platforms?

4. Do you understand the production process for the product you are designing for well enough not to run into issues with the creative director?

5. If your design work is going overseas, have you worked with overseas printing and manufacturing processes?

6. If you can, figure out a way to reach out in person at places like a wholesale trade show. This will make you a warm lead and help you stand out from all the designers sending emails.

7. Can you handle lots of "no's"? If you have a thick enough skin, trying repeatedly and accepting rejection is a great way to find a contract.

8. Do you have connections in the industry that will help make the manufacturers warm leads for you?

If you are a designer with everything on this list, your likelihood of getting a contract becomes greater. If you miss even one thing, it may be the difference between getting or losing that contract.

The other way you can make money is by producing products yourself. I have done this a few different ways but the first time it was with physical sewing patterns. I remember creating the four patterns, getting them printed, and then…well, crickets. This is because I didn't understand the distribution process for these products. Through trial and error, I figured out how to sell those patterns. But it took learning a whole new skill set in distribution.

If you go the physical product route, know exactly how you sell those products. Then test that method to see if it works. I know plenty of people who have spent $100,000 on products that then sit in their basements. That's because they were way more excited to make the product than to learn how to sell it. It's an expensive lesson, so tread carefully if you create and manufacture your own products.

Carina's 2015 Apricot & Persimmon
Collection and 2018 Eek Book Shriek
Collection for Riley Blake Designs

(right) Carina's Eek Boo Shriek eBook

# CHAPTER 10

MAKE A PLAN

I have laid out several models throughout this book to help you win as a designer, but ironically, most people will never do any of them.

This is why this chapter is about creating a plan.

At a Design Suite Live Retreat, I dedicated about thirty minutes to creating an individualized, hour-by-hour plan with two members. One was a stay-at-home mom. The other was a working mom. Once we isolated their actual free time, we broke down that time with realistic timelines and breaks for implementation, production, and sales.

A detailed plan like this gives designers a realistic picture of what can be accomplished daily, weekly, and yearly. It also allows them to understand more about how quickly they can accumulate products in their shops and how fast they will make money.

There is a myth that artists and designers thrive in chaotic craziness. Because of this myth, creatives think they can go forth, create, and be free. It is a lovely idea but it will not build you a business.

I do believe there should be some creative chaos in a design business, but that creative chaos should happen within a well-formed plan.

For many years, I would have a booth at Quilt Market for my fabric designs. I would get sample yardage a few weeks before the show to create quilts and apparel for my booth. It was a mad dash to get everything done. I had a tiny house and shared an office with my toddler's crib. Often, I would fly my mom in to help me sew and projects would be laid out on every floor in the house. My kids would step carefully over half-cut-out dresses with pins in them in the kitchen or jump over a big mound of projects barricading the living room. Through it all, we had a schedule for what needed to be finished and how long we had to do it. It was chaotic, but there was a plan.

The key to building a great plan is building in small but easy deadlines each day. I do this with all of my design deadlines. As I write this book, I am working on a fabric collection, a new wallpaper collection, and new prints. Each of them has deadlines on my calendar and individual daily deadlines to make sure I hit the big one.

To make money, planning is an essential element of your design business. Determine how many products you need and schedule the time to make them. Many amazing potential designers have fallen into the trap of not planning their design time. The result is a lack of production time and sales. This eats into your profits as a designer.

In year one, I push my new designers to do minimal or no social media. Becoming fast and proficient in design software is important in planning your time. There is a truth that all designers need to embrace. It is, "Everything takes longer than you think it will." Yes, plan for that!

Deadlines

When I was the Creative Director at Cartabella, I was always under a deadline. The biggest wholesale show of the year was always in January, which meant December was a crazy month.

I also had my third baby in my first year as the Creative Director. He was about 5 months old in December, so my schedule was an amazing mess. I switched between the new baby, two small children, production work on all the lines, catalog creation, website management, and final approvals.

After that month, I told myself I would never live my life like that again (and thankfully, I have kept that promise to myself), but it taught me that I worked better under a hard deadline. If I know there is an end to a project, I am more likely to push through to finish it.

While I hope you never go through a crazy season like I did, I know there are many of you reading this book juggling multiple things. Some of you are caring for children. You may take care of aging parents. Some of you have a full-time job and want to transition into design. I work with designers with disabilities. Perhaps you are fighting against a difficult disease, illness, or mental health issue.

While I have not experienced all of these things, I have experienced some difficult things that allow me to empathize with your situation.

Here is the good news. I have also seen designers from all walks of life succeed in this field despite difficult circumstances. Because of this, I believe anyone can be a designer if they get help to make it happen.

I want you to succeed at this, which means putting a plan in place. No matter where you are creating your design business, finish this chapter and write a plan. Need help with this? I have planning pages in the workbook that you can download for free that goes with this book at www.designprofitprosperbook.com.

My Personal Plan

Creating a business plan is maybe the most important piece of the design, profit, and prosper puzzle. How will you ever become a designer if you never create a plan incorporating design into your daily life?

How do I like to plan? I am pragmatic and like to break down my daily activities. Pretty simple, right?

I find that building solid deadlines helps me succeed. I love a weekly deadline and daily deadlines. My favorite weekly deadline was Friday afternoon, when I designed full-time.

Part of the reason I had a Friday deadline was that one of my shops only allowed me to submit a certain number of designs each week. I would lose those listings if I didn't get my products in. This was a brilliant strategy from the online shop because it ensured that their designers turned in designs. Many online shops do not have deadlines. Because of this, designers are sporadic about their product posting.

This is how you will be different. You will post weekly at a minimum because you will give yourself a solid deadline. It does not matter when your deadline is (mine in recent years turned into Saturday at 7 am). For some of my designers, Monday at noon or Thursday at 10 pm works well. The deadline doesn't matter. Having one does.

This deadline will dictate all the other activities of the week. This is where the Design Process Model comes in handy. Because my deadline is at the end of the week, I generally spend the first few days in implementation. So Monday, Tuesday, and Wednesday, I am dedicated to creating design work.

My Thursday was almost always devoted to production. I would test files, make educational videos, and compress products.

Friday, I committed to sales. For my online shops, that included uploading products to my various websites, SEO, and descriptions. If I was looking for a contract, that was the day I would research companies, book wholesale shows, and send emails. If I were building a freelance network, I would send emails and upload them to an agency website.

The Design Process Model™ In One Possible Daily Plan

This specific plan does not work for everyone. For example, if I worked a full-time job, I might instead use all five days of the business week for creating design work because I had less time every day to do it. Then I would use Saturday for production and sales.

I also have designers whom I have advised to build their implementation time and production time into the same day. An example of this would be to spend Monday, Tuesday, Wednesday, and Thursday doing implementation and production. Friday would then be dedicated to sales.

It does not matter how you structure your time, as long as you give each thing enough time in your plan.

You will notice I didn't plan a day for ideation. Most designers tend to be visionaries, so I find that ideation is happening all the time. If you need ideation time, create short spurts of timed research time so that thirty minutes does not turn into three hours on social media or google. Many visionaries do not put a time limit on their "research," which means all those precious hours that should have been spent in designing are instead spent on imagining things.

Limit your ideation time and emphasize the *doing* in your business. This means spending most of your time as an operator in your business. This is also why planning is so important. If you mark down what time you will spend in implementation, production, and sales, you will actually do it. Everyday activities you do as a designer will make you *feel* like a designer. This is an important part of transitioning from hobbyist to designer for new designers. Designing every day gives us the activities that prove we are designers. This will improve your confidence and skills.

Planning is a fun way to see what I can accomplish. In my program Design Suite, our first Virtual Conference of every year is dedicated to annual design planning. It is exciting to see how many products you can produce and how many designs you can make. If you view planning as an exciting way to implement an amazing design business, it will take you far.

But remember, it is time to *do it* once you *plan it.*

Why The Design Process Model Works for Planners

Early on, as a designer, I would spend all of my time, you know, designing. By doing so, I would then run into Friday frantically trying to figure out how to market my products and sell them.

By adding a full day in production (because production always takes more time than I think it will) and a day for sales, I am dividing my time in a way that makes more sense. I did not love the frantic rush on Friday, which then pushed into Saturday or Sunday because I didn't finish the final vital steps of the Design Process. Zipping files, checking the color mode, and cleaning up my art board always took longer than I expected it to.

Using the Design Process model to plan out your days or week, you can see where you spend most of your time. Is most of your time spent in ideation? It's time to take hours away from that. Are you spending little time on sales? Give it more room so you can write out descriptions, emails, and SEO with time to spare.

The most compelling reason for having a plan is that I love to wake up fresh on a Monday morning, ready to start working on a new set of ideas. That fresh start makes designing a rewarding creative experience for me.

I am frustrated if I have production and sales whipping into my Monday because I didn't finish them during the previous week. When I plan well, this does not happen.

Carina's die cuts for multiple online shops

# CHAPTER 11
CONSISTENCY

Throughout this book, I have tried to help you see that to profit as a designer, you will need to become different by becoming an exceptional designer, and if you can plan out the design process in your everyday life, you can succeed.

While this seems very simple, many designers will start and become disillusioned with the process in a few weeks or months. That's because it takes *more* time, *more* effort, and *more* conviction than most people will follow through with to create a successful design business. Of course there is also the daunting task of jumping all three hurdles simultaneously or even at one time.

It will take you more hours, practice, and strategy to make this dream of becoming a profitable designer come true. Creativity comes with a cost. But the cost is worthwhile. I would rather work hard in a creative career than do some hard or boring desk job any day. It is the consistent, boring work of production and sales that creates stellar design businesses. This is because creativity and differentiation come with consistency.

Part of how you will stand out from the crowd of designers is by seeking better strategies, the inside scoop of design knowledge, and staying in the design game longer than everyone else.

This is how you will become profitable. You are going to find that Sweet Spot.

One of my Design Suite members stated that in one of her shops, she had about 100 products and the stats showed that her shop was doing better than 90% of the other shops.

Based on this, it takes a lot less effort than most designers realize to be in the top ten percent because many new designers never get far enough along to have enough products to get a reasonable number of sales. This shows that most new designers drop off before seeing much success.

One of my shops was like this as well. I had a relatively low sales rate in this shop, but it showed I was in the top 5% of shops selling. I believe this shop was making less than $200 a month, but I was making more sales than 95% of the shops out there. That's astonishing.

I sometimes talk about the fear of the design industry being an over saturated place. Aspiring designers fear there is no room for them. The stats repeatedly show that the market isn't over saturated with designers. It is over saturated with hobbyists or "starters."

A hobbyist or a starter dabbles. They love designing but they are not committed to it. They do not put time on the calendar to design and they do not design daily. They rarely make time for production or sales. They do *what feels good.*

Now there are lots of times in my business when things feel good. But I cannot afford to do just what feels good. If that were the case, I would spend every day thinking about great designs and drawing.

I am committed to creating a design business, and you should be too. Designers who commit to a business will follow through, consistently design, consistently sell, and work for long-term goals.

Designers willing to put in a lot of work, especially at the beginning, will see results that others will not see.

A Word About Volume

I have minimum standards for my designers in my product design program. That's because I spent years working towards a high product goal. This does several things, including the following.

1. By choosing several products to produce each week, you will perform consistently.

2. Many online shops have "new" sections where designers can get featured when they upload weekly.

3. Some online shops have algorithms that benefit those that upload more often.

4. By producing many products, you find your style much faster.

5. You get faster in the software by producing a larger number of products.

Your product output will depend on your current situation. I would advise a young mother differently than a working woman. Always the standard should be to push yourself to make as many products as possible.

The volume of product is one of the most important keys to the profit equation.

Here's how I know that most designers do not understand how much product they must produce to succeed. I once had a consult with an aspiring designer who told me she had 200 products in a particular shop. With all sincerity, she felt this was a large number of products and could not understand why she did not have many sales.

I knew well the strategies for making money in the shop she was in. She did not understand that 200 was a small number of designs for that shop. This meant she probably spent a lot of her time in ideation and implementation but had spent little time on sales strategy. I quickly checked into that shop and realized that her numbers were nowhere near what they had to be to make money.

I find that most designers feel that 200, 500 or even 1000 designs means they should have made it already. They do not understand just how much you must make or how quickly you must make it to be successful.

If you are a seasoned designer, think back to your first designs. I know my first designs were not that good even **AFTER** finishing graduate degrees. They are nothing like the products I create now. This means that the products I made around the 200 mark were simply not as good as the ones I made at the 5000 mark.

As a designer, your goal is to **STRETCH** yourself to become the best. This includes the number of products you produce. Amping up your production numbers is how you profit and prosper.

Using the Good Better Best Model

Determine how to get the most out of the Good Better Best Model in your business. Remind yourself that you are on a design journey. Do not be one of those designers who expect to be an overnight sensation.

From personal experience, it takes years, if not decades, to figure out best practices in your business. While each designer and business are unique, one thing remains consistent. The best designers are profitable because they stand out. They desire to make beautiful, highly functional products.

Be okay with it taking longer than you think to make your design business go. Also be open to learning to become better through designing every day. Remember you are jumping hurdles as you become better everyday!

Initially, your designs will be good. That is okay because you are learning. By creating all those "good" products, learning the production on them, and selling them, you will create a wealth of experience for yourself that will turn you into a better and best designer.

This takes time and effort because of those darn hurdles.

But you can do it.

You have only to plan out the time for every step of your design process to make it happen.

Using the Design Process Model

I love teaching this process in my boot camps and workshops because it is a great way for designers to figure out what is important and how to plan their time. Stick to this model to build a solid foundation in your business. It will serve you well.

I recently worked on a set of sticker sheets, and I identified all the steps in the process. I had an idea. I then sat down and laid out my stickers on an 8.5 in. x 11 in. sheet of paper. I made die lines for those stickers as I ensured that everything looked great together because I know the key to a great sticker sheet is to make it look full and dynamic. Then I took a few minutes to ensure all the die lines were the correct lines and colors. I ensured that I rasterized the images so they were all on a single layer. When all the production work was done, I waited until the next day, when I uploaded several products at the same time. I wrote up descriptions, linked the instructions, and put in some keywords. With that, sales were done.

I go through my Design Process daily and weekly. If you are finding yourself in the Design Process cycle and finishing all four steps, then you will start winning before you know it.

The designers who are not winning are leaving out one of those steps.

Using the 3 Hurdles To Your Advantage

One of the key advantages of recognizing that there are three hurdles is that you will be paying attention as you design and jumping those hurdles as you go. You find yourself asking the questions, "Have I mastered the software?", "Is this design different or stylistic enough?", and "Am I getting the experience I need to move forward?"

This self awareness will make you a better designer and allow you to glide through some of the rough patches that all designers go through.

You Are Worthy of A Creative Life

I know I have not touched on this final topic much in this book because I wanted to fill it with actionable steps to help you think about ways to become profitable. Some of you will read this book and get a picture of what it will take to become a designer. Some of you will read this book and feel a hope that you have not felt for a long time. Some of you will read this book and get into the weeds of worry of how you will do all of these things fast enough.

It does not matter how you feel about the different models or steps. The thing I need you to understand is that if you have wanted to become a designer, you CAN become a designer.

You are worthy and deserving of a beautiful, creative life.

To get there will take strength, ingenuity, and—above all else—creativity. After all, you want to become a designer. Becoming a designer means looking for the creative solutions that others will not come up with. Your willingness to do the work and think differently will help you build a successful business that will allow you to open your eyes everyday excited for what the day will bring you.

My designers consistently tell me that they wake up knowing that they are living their dream, making money, and are excited for what the day has in store for them.

That is powerful, intentional living. It is designing, profiting, and prospering.

Resources

Download the free workbook for this book at
www.designprofitprosperbook.com.

Learn about my design work in fabric, paper, digital, courses, and
more at www.carinagardner.com.

I also referenced Jenny Doan's book *How To Stitch An American Dream*
in the first chapter. I laughed, I cried, and I cannot recommend it
enough.

Hang out with me on instagram at @carinagardner for design and
@carinagardnerinkclub for paper crafting.

Get more design advice on youtube.com/carinagardner and the
Make and Design with Carina Gardner podcast.

Acknowledgments

A heartfelt thank you to my designers in Design Suite. This book was written for you. Every word was meant to help you continue to succeed in making your dreams come true. Every time you post your sales and wins, it feels like I have won too. Thank you to each of you for letting me be a part of your journey and a part of your success. Keep dreaming big!

A huge thank you to the Carina Gardner, Inc. Team. It is a privilege to work with a team that works so hard to help designers around to world achieve their dreams. Your hard work and talent does not go unnoticed.

A big thank you to my husband Josh, who helped edit the book and pushed the button on the camera to take every picture for this book or my website. Your support has helped me achieve my own design dreams for over 20 years. Thank you for your everlasting support and love.

To my entrepreneurial girlfriends who let me dream as big as I want and believe in me in ways I never expected. Thank you for being a part of my growth journey!

To my mentors along the way. I believe mentorship has the potential to change your life because I know it changed mine! To Lee Ellen Beach, my high school speech teacher who taught me to have confidence. To Barbara Martinson, who headed my masters and doctoral committee. I had the great pleasure to learn how to teach design from her. To Stacy Tushl, who helped me better understand how to run my own businesses.

Thank you to Susan Harbin and Ravi Ramigati for their contributions to this book.

Finally to my children. They have watched me go after my goals, and I'm grateful for their encouragement and support. Felicity once said I was very "determined" and I think I took that to heart. I feel lucky to be your mom, Siri, Felicity, and Charlie! I love you so much!

About the Author

Carina has a Ph.D. in Design from the University of Minnesota. She taught design at the University of Minnesota for five years before starting Carina Gardner, Inc.

Carina was also the Creative Director of Cartabella Scrapbooking. The Carina Gardner brand has been on dishware, jewelry, prints, and holiday products for Deseret Book. Her brand Mini Lou has been featured in Nordstrom, Peek Clothing, and 500 independent retailers and museums in the US.

Carina currently designs fabric for Riley Blake Designs, die cut files for Silhouette, and multiple online stores. She is the Creative Director of Design Suite Agency, which exclusively features designers from her Design Suite program.

Tutorials on quilting, crafting, and design can be found on her YouTube channel at www.youtube.com/carinagardner. Her wallpaper collections and print collections are showcased on her short term rental series on YouTube which began April 2023.

Carina teaches surface pattern and crafting design in her high level mastermind called Design Suite. Design Suite is the only design education online program that teaches designers how to make money as they learn to design. You can learn more about Carina's programs, bootcamps, and workshops at carinagardnercourses.com.

Her podcast—Make and Design with Carina Gardner—airs three times a week anywhere you listen to podcasts.

Carina is originally from Clarksville, Tennessee. Carina currently lives in Sandy, Utah with her husband, three children, two cats, and a dog.

Made in the USA
Las Vegas, NV
01 March 2024

86561917R00075